I0419701

DIRTY POLITICS:
BOKO HARAM
IN
PERSPECTIVE

MARXX WELLS

Guudcence Publishing, Inc.
...*beyond frontiers*™

DEDICATION

This work is dedicated to all the dead and misplaced victims of Islamic terrorism and unrest worldwide. May your pains bear the fruition of a world with the will to checkmate the rise and spread of jihadist ideals.

"Sons of Islam everywhere, the jihad is a duty – to establish the rule of Allah on earth and to liberate your countries and yourselves from America's domination and its Zionist allies. It is your battle – either victory or martyrdom."

-Ahmed Yassin

CONTENTS

INTRODUCTION

The name Nigeria was coined by an English journalist, Miss Flora Shaw, in an article in the London Times of January 8, 1897 – describing the land of the River Niger. But who coined the name Zamfara is unknown, as is which of the two – the river or the land – preceded the other in being called so.

Ancient Zamfara and modern Zamfara, do not in all facets share an identical geography, let alone a historical and or a political identity. The binding link between the two however, stems from the modern having much of its land circumscribed within the borders of the ancient – a situation that presents an overlap in the geographical, historical and political definition of the twain, i.e. the old and the new.

The sole objective of this work is the presentation of a lucid literature; premised on offering a well-rounded insight into the bludgeoning Islamist perpetrated unrest clearly evident in 21st century Northern Nigeria. This is meritorious because such violence, killing and maiming threatens to destabilize the entire sub-region of West Africa – with the ripple effect of markedly rendering the world unsafe. It is, first, a cogent treatise of Zamfara in her struggle for self-determination on the secular demographic esplanade of modernity. Secondly, it is a factual dissertation of the subtle reasons underlying the clamor for self-determination. Thirdly, it proffers a bird's-eye view to the jihadists' agitations rocking the political landscape of northern Nigeria and the formidable Boko Haram agenda seeking to overthrow democracy for the institution of Islamist ideals while attempting to set up yet another caliphate in sub-Saharan Africa.

Achieving this objective, especially with regards to the historical compendium of Zamfara, given the complex jigsaws that dent the available oral traditions and chronicles of this subject has not been without headaches. Indeed, the daily exasperating task of weeding out discrepancies that habitually threaten to thwart this effort has been a subtle art most demanding, but equally rewarding.

It is true that great hiatuses exist in every period, giving rise to many obscurities in the histories of these times. For Zamfara and indeed Western Sudan, not only are these gulfs present, wars of conquests and dynastic upheavals have caused the depletion and outright destruction of historical documents of crucial importance. Thus, ancient Zamfara is an ambiguous entity on the pages of pre-Islamic Negro Africa. Most of the oral traditions purporting to be representative of the histories of these times are no more than mere mythical expositions. And these tall tales have had the pedestrian vulnerability of being subjected to crass distortions – after all, who said myth is an astute preserver of concrete historical episodes? If anything, they do indeed have an affiliation with institutions that have/had their nucleus in historical origins, but with the passage of time have acquired the undesirable airs of interpolation, reformation, suppression, a little exaggeration here and there, and the eventual transmutation of the very ordinary into the miraculous – by which time it is nearly impossible to decipher the counterfeit from the genuine.

Then there are the frequent periods of eclipse when the city-state had no legitimate ruler, coupled with a constant relocation of the city-state headquarters, such that the historical data of relevance of these times are at best much too fragmentary and unrelated to lend worthwhile significance to the events credited to these periods. Here, eulogistic antithetical oral traditions contending on equal footing with documented chronicles of reliability are relegated into the trash cans of folklore – apologies to the oral tradition apologists.

On the whole, these ambiguous format of data of the ancient cropped up from the absence of a dominant continuous geopolitical unity to give the adequate cogency needed to the meager, often times total absence, most times plain unreliability of original sources, and then too, the aggressive inequality of material available. A situation aggravated by the people of this land, the Hausa, easily one of the largest linguistic groups within the perimeters circumscribing Negro Africa.

The problems posed by this lot are inherent, because although having a common language, they did not in any way form an ethnic unity. Affiliation based on a common Lingua Franca ran surprisingly only skin deep: Affiliation based on immediate geography/clan being the more potent.

In endeavoring to write with merciless accuracy, a seeming bias has been apportioned to pro-Islamic data on the history of Zamfara. This is because it is one that can be conveniently dealt with in the scathing light of austere truth while dealing with subjects that are wont to brand you as a facilitator for Islamophobic awakenings. Also, the regular romance with the histories of other kingdoms have been necessary because once the herculean process of city-state establishment had been attained, Zamfara fell into some kind of limbo, with proof of her existence to be found only in the histories of other neighboring states. Proofs accentuated only when the latter had any occasion of major brushes with the former.

In the long run, the historical compendium of ancient Zamfara has relied more on selection rather than detail. This has often been necessary, as earlier explained, warranting that some disproportion of treatment has been regrettably unavoidable. The result of the whole history is, therefore, a kind of chronological anthology having the paraphernalia of a mosaic built up into some form of coherent sequence in a bold attempt to harmonize the conflicting juxtaposition of varied material. It does some good to the history of Zamfara and sets the stage for understanding the looping influence it's had on the agenda of Boko Haram: The yawning mimicry of erstwhile postulates, ideals and aspirations is all too glaring to ignore.

1 PRE-JIHAD ZAMFARA

No matter how heavily the odds weighed against them, there was no turning back now. In the throes of minting their deeds on the never fading tablets of history, no price was too high. Such was the monolithic essence of their determination in the face of the dire pangs of thirst and hunger, and the severe violence of feelings – no thanks to a blazing, unblinking sun.

For a disarrayed formation of men armed with no more than cudgels to lay claim to a land with or without occupiers in the wake of the formidable obstacles of nature is not a task for the faint-hearted! But success, they say, favors the daring. Besides, going by the fatalistic beliefs of nearly 1.6 billion Muslims, these tribesmen exuding perseverance equaled only by the fervor of religious duty were no more than pawns on the inscrutable field of providence.

By the 12th century AD, the city-state of Zamfara was a tangible entity in Western Sudan; spanning from the range of the arc described by the River Rima in the north to the River Ka downwards due southwest. This tangible entity started off first as a walled village after the tribesmen had emerged victorious in their conquest to claim the land. The walls made the markings of a geographical divide enclosing a large area of an open self-sufficient community complete with trade and industry. Also available was a large area of open land for cultivation. All these features enabled its inhabitants to support a long siege. People from other surrounding hamlets came within its walls when hostile armies threatened, as was often the case. Gradually, the status of a city-state was achieved when the village-state secured the acknowledgement of a widening circle of hamlets and then of neighboring village-states (usually by the dual strategy of colonization after conquest or by granting protection from enemies from farther away). Soon a capital town at Dutsi (in present day Zurmi Local Government Area) emerged whose head, the *Sarki* changed from a nondescript village-head to a pompous city-chief in control of an elaborate court and official hierarchy. The other walled villages of the confederation became subordinate chieftaincies. With the progress of time, political unity began to take on spirituality for enhanced cohesion, embodied in the foundation myth with the apt introduction of regal deities, taboos, and rituals.

The first tribesmen that occupied the land, the *Zamfarawa*, were Hausa. They were later joined by the Fulanis who formed scattered enclaves all over the territory. The Fulanis recognized the suzerainty of the Hausas and the two lived in symbiosis, as was the case throughout Hausaland. With time, the Fulanis intermarried with the Hausa and took on Hausa language and customs for the most part. So also the repeated invasion of Zamfara land by the Katsinawa, Kebbawa and Gobirawa brought enclaves of these Hausa tribes into Zamfara. Together these have evolved into a unity of ethnic bloc, Zamfarawa, which does not recognize any of the various ethnic blocs that cast it into its present mold.

No one is quite sure of whom the first ruler of the Zamfarawa was. Postulations about their very roots are also blurred. What we do have on record is that Bukurukuru is the first regent to make an appearance into the pages of history as a ruler of the Zamfarawa. An appearance made in 1300AD when he is noted to have founded Birnin[1] Zamfara near the present town of Isa in Sokoto state. What remains of Birnin Zamfara is still visible close to the eastern entrance of Isa town. Presumably, therefore, the rulers before Bukurukuru were not *sarakuna*[2] but clan heads (much the same way a man heads his family), and thus pre-dynastic figures.

Perhaps the sole reason for Bukurukuru's emergence into the fore pages of Zamfara's history is the pomp he is said to have displayed during his era – surrounding himself with as much ostentation as was possible within the limits of his "enormous" wealth. Instead of consolidating his domain at a time when the realm between the Niger and the Chad, divided into little states, dwelt in mutual enmity more than half the time, and at times paying allegiance to the greater states of the east (Kanem Bornu) and west (Songhai), he engaged in an unnecessary fanfare of extravagance which culminated in the transfer of the kingdom's capital from Dutsi to Birnin Zamfara.

Panjandrum Bukurukuru's demise ushered in the enthronement of a number of rulers to whom very little is credited. Yargoje, a queen, fourth in succession to the throne of Zamfara after Bukurukuru, is the ruler next most accounted for. Her reign spanned the better parts of an age of four decades. During her era, she relocated the capital from Birnin Zamfara to Dan[3] Sadau, however for reasons of safety rather than seeking vain-glory. The wall she erected for added protection, and to mark the extremities of her capital, stands today metamorphosed, providing an attraction for tourists to Dan Sadau. A lamp, purportedly hers, is also on display at the Sokoto State History Bureau.

Although the advent of Bayajidda, a prince of Bagdad, into Western Sudan stamped patrilineal succession to the throne (with exclusive rights only for males), most heathen enclaves still maintained the age-old, essentially traditional matrilineal pattern that had characterized pre-early half of the 14th century AD; as evidenced by the reign of Yargoje sometime from 1350 AD.

Yargoje, and indeed subsequent rulers, were unable to raise Zamfara to the attainment of the rank of a kingdom or empire like those of Katsina, Kano or Zaria, although these kingdoms were themselves insignificant when compared to the greatness of Ghana, Mali or Songhai empires (in the west) and Kanem Bornu (in the east). They lacked the essential warlord disposition that many times saw to the rapid expansion of city-states via annexations.

While the rulers of Zamfara were busy playing safe, Islam, the colonizing religion, was fast gaining in-roads into the domains governed by indigenous traditions.

Islam, indeed, is said to have made its novel appearance in West Africa at Takrur, a kingdom on both sides of the River Senegal. This was before 1000AD. The people of Takrur are the Toucouleurs and Fulanis. From the 12th century AD onward, some Fulanis, being a nomadic tribe by nature, wandered from their home base at Takrur, spreading all over West Africa from Senegal to the Cameroons in search of pasture for their ever growing livestock population. Takrur is most probably the same as Futa-Toro in today's Senegal; a place where the Fulanis are first mentioned in history. Thus, by 1400AD, Islam had already registered its presence in Hausaland. But whether or not its introduction was by the Wangarawa (a Fulani tribe) from the west or by the Kanem-Bornus from the east is uncertain, and certainly debatable. And it was not until 1463 to 1499 during the reign of Mohammad Rimfa of Kano that Islam first got institutionalized into the state affairs of Hausaland. Katsina, a kingdom very close to Zamfara due northeast, got Islam during the reign of Ibrahim Maje (1494-1520). All these while, however, Gobir, Zamfara, Yauri and Zaria remained predominantly pagan, possibly due to their non-contact or minimal exposure to Muslim traders.

Mohammad Kanta, a mercenary, emigrating from Ibrahim Maje's Katsina to Kebbi in search of adventure and fortune, enlisted into *Askiya's*[4] army, lending his genius at warfare to the services of *Askiya* Mohammad. At this time, Kebbi, Zamfara, Katsina and Kano were all tribute-paying principalities of the empire ruled by *Askiya* Mohammad (1493-1528). In 1517, during the reign of Mawashi dan Bardan of Zamfara, Kanta staged a revolt against the *Askiya*, teaming up with the Kebbawa with whom he now claimed natal ties – over the sharing of the spoils of war against the Azbinawa of Niger. The revolt was an immense success, affording the Kebbawa under the "indigenous" leadership of Mohammad Kanta the long-sought opportunity to declare themselves independent. Mohammad Kanta then built a formidable army in readiness for any eventual reprisal from the *Askiya* – made up of a cavalry of horsemen and camel riders, putting to effective use the spoils and loot he had acquired from the consequence of secession.

Between 1450-1530, Hausaland was the bone of contention between the Kanem-Bornu and the Songhai empires, each seeking to colonize as much of this vast land as possible. Mohammad Kanta, now governing an independent state, soon joined the scramble. Wangara, a commercially important and powerful domain (its king having a standing army of about seven hundred thousand archers and five hundred horsemen) lying southwest of Zamfara came under the threat of Mohammad Kanta in his unbridled quest for more power and land at the same time when the *Mai*[5] of Kanem-Bornu also had his eyes on this town. It was a gloomy affair for Wangara. But momentarily they basked in vain relief when the latter abandoned his attempt of conquest in consequence of war with the Prince of Gaoje. In alliance with Katsina, Mohammad Kanta seized this perfect opportunity to claim Wangara. It disappeared, along with large parts of Zamfara, absorbed by Kanta and Katsina. Kigaya Tubaran Dan Taskarinburan, regent of Zamfara during this war, had failed Zamfara by thinking it safer to play the onlooker in these times when every

4

acknowledged city-state sought some form of dominance over its neighbors via active participation in conquest. Unwittingly he played Zamfara into the waiting hands of the others. Anyway, Zamfara still survived as a city-state despite losing some of its territory to Kanta and Katsina, thanks to an unaffected capital, Birnin Zamfara.

A very smart ruler, Kanta chose to leave the day-to-day governance of annexed principalities in the hands of their own chiefs so as to check unnecessary disaffection while concentrating his attention on consolidating his state by further conquests. In today's political parlance, what he did is referred to as "indirect rule". So, he was content, after the capture of a territory, to obtain a treaty of subjectivity and allegiance in the form of payment of taxes to him. At the zenith of his influence, he built a capital at Surame, his "native" district, along with other powerful fortresses nearby, viz. Birnin Leka and Gungu. The citadel of his base was therefore in the western extremities of Hausaland. The Fulanis were to choose the same region for their twin capitals of Sokoto and Gwandu ages later. Present Birnin Kebbi at this time was a resting station for tired merchants on their way to Surame and Gungu. Argungu was not yet founded.

Askiya Mohammad Bengan, feeling belittled by the successes of Mohammad Kanta, decided to attack him. He suffered a humiliating defeat at the hands of Kanta that saw to the further decline of his empire already impoverished by the Moroccan conquest. In 1545 during the reign of Fatifati dan Kigaya of Zamfara, the *Mai* of Kanem-Bornu, Ali-ibn[6]-Idris, also decided to curb the powers of the fast growing kingdom of Kebbi by waging war on her. The battle having ensued was driven all the way to Surame, capital of Kanta's Kebbi. Clearly his forces were no match for the *Mai's* superior army. Only by employing the tactics of trickery was the impending defeat of Kebbi averted. Using the decoy of rooting the dead among them carrying bows and arrows, ready to be fired, made to appear to be laughing scared the superstitious Kanem-Bornu invading army into flight. In flight the Kebbawa slew them by the multitudes, pursuing them far off east to Nguru in Bornu Empire. Here, the Kanem-Bornu, realizing their folly, made a desperate stand to reclaim victory that was far too long lost. The battle turned out eventually to be Kanta's boldest conquest ever; like a phoenix, he had risen from the ashes of near defeat to unprecedented victory. Unfortunately, while returning home to Surame, this brave Field

Marshal was waylaid by common bandits from Katsina and murdered in cold blood. The demise of this illustrious leader of Kebbi marked the resurgence of Zamfara into the forefronts of Hausaland history again. A resurgence that saw Taritu dan Kigaya (successor to Fatifati) struggling to keep together the principalities that made up the confederate city-states of Zamfara in the face of bloodletting feuds that had overtaken its neighbors.

Askiya Daud was clever enough to realize that the kingdom of Kebbi was too much established to be defied by conquest. However, his counterpart at Kebbi, seeking cheap fame and not as smart as Mohammad Kanta, engaged in small and meaningless conquests that soon generated into an open confrontation with *Askiya* Daud. A confrontation in which Daud preferred to play defensive until 1552 when it was probable that he could have overrun Kebbi had he chosen to play offensive. In 1553 the ruler of Kebbi (now employing the name *Kanta* for official title) sued for peace. *Askiya* Daud complied. Eight years later, in 1561, this unruly *Kanta* died, after deflating the importance of his kingdom.

All this while Zamfara was yet to assimilate Islam into its cultural ways of life; the way neighboring states had. And it was not until 1640 that it first boasted of a Muslim leader, Aliyu dan Daka dan Fatifati dan Kigaya, and a pathetic form of institutionalized Islam: The populace professed Islam but openly indulged in the practice of pagan rituals. But for Islam a triumph had been scored, because although the 17th century AD registered a grave decline of Islam in Western Sudan in general, it was during this time that the city-state of Zamfara embraced Islam en masse, albeit without the formal introduction of the Shari'a.

The successors of Mohammad Kanta were only able to maintain power over the surrounding states for barely half a century. Perhaps, if they had been able to hang onto it for a little longer and more firmly, they just might have been able to build upon the foundation already laid a power capable of rivaling that of Kanem-Bornu. But the opposite was the case. Their grip on power was so slippery that soon (in the 1670s) *Sarkin* Zamfara, Suleiman dan Abdu na[7] Bawanka, *Sarkin* Gobir, Mohammad ibn Ciroma and *Sarkin* Ahir, Agada ibn Mohammad, dared to rise up against Kebbi, defeating her in the event. Each of these chiefs took possession of the lands which were nearest to him. *Sarkin* Zamfara was able to reclaim as well as annex more lands than the other chiefs. Having tasted the invigorating euphoria of success, the Zamfarawa maintained a sustained aggression on Kebbi even under Mohammad na Makake dan Abdu na Bawanka, the next regent. The principal cities of Kebbi (Surame and Gungu) was eventually ruined by Babba I dan Mohammad na Makake. This bitter defeat by the Zamfarawa, a people only recently uninterested in the regional power-plays, led to the abandonment of Surame in 1715 and the building of Birnin Kebbi as the new capital of the Kebbawa by the Fulani some time later.

By the middle of the 18th century AD Zamfara under Gado dan Gibama (1748-1754) was the leading power of the Rima River valley. Its expansionist conquests in the previous years had pushed its borders further; from Sabon Birni in the north to Kuyambana in the south, Muniya and Rubu in the east to Rafin Gindi in the west. The limelight Zamfara now enjoyed by virtue of its prominence prompted the Gobirawa expelled from Gora Rima in Niger to seek asylum from Maroki dan Malu (1754-17?). Their stay as guests of the ruler of Zamfara was shot lived. After managing to obtain by scheming, the cult secrets of the Zamfarawa, they sacked Birnin Zamfara and established their capital at Alkalawa, twenty-five miles from Birnin Zamfara in 1759 under the prompting of Babari their leader. In 1764 the Zamfara dynasty was forced into exile. Maroki settled at Kiyawa and by his presence rendered Kiyawa the new capital of a much disorganized and disoriented confederation. But Kiyawa did not prove to be the safe haven he had hoped to find solace in from the embarrassment of defeat. The Gobirawa, determined to erase any thing that could lead to a coordinated vendetta from the Zamfarawa, destroyed Kiyawa in a battle during which Maroki chose to commit suicide rather than face another round of humiliation. Again, the capital had been lost. And with it came an interregnum of four decades. Zamfara had become eclipsed by the rising power of Gobir. The reason for the "untimely" decline of Zamfara was its failure to make the much needed politico-military stance that would have made it an empire of repute. So weak was it in this regard that before its defeat by the Gobirawa it had in spite of its leading role in the Rima River valley become a tribute-paying state with allegiance pledged to the *Mai* of Kanem-Bornu.

The sacking of the Zamfarawa from their capital town of Birnin

Zamfara, and the subsequent incessant harassments did not, however, spell a complete obliteration of the kingdom. In fact when Bawa Jan Gwarzo rose to the throne of Gobir at Alkalawa after the demise of Babari during Zamfara's interregnum period, Zamfara sought to claim back some of its lost lands. The efforts failed. Bawa Jan Gwarzo was too astute a ruler for the feeble uprisings to climax into any real threat. And by having the entire members of the Zamfarawa dynasty thrown into prison he checkmated any thoughts of further uprisings.

Jan Gwarzo established the monarchy of Gobir by instituting its sovereignty in his bold refusal to continue the payment of tax due to the *Mai* of Bornu, as his predecessor Babari, in conjunction with other Hausa states of Western Sudan, had been doing: Songhai Empire no longer enjoyed the privilege, having lost its political influence by its decline. His tenure however, was plagued by general discontent of his subjects, and Islam was been impudently used only as a veneer to gain acceptance. The elite could not help pandering to indigenous animistic beliefs; neither did they lend their voice against the endemic misrule perpetuated. A misrule that found expression in the heavy and unjust taxes imposed upon the citizens. Thus, these unsavory situations were to eventually inspire the momentous "reformatory" incidence of Uthman dan Fodio's jihad. Both Muslims and non-Muslim elements, Fulani and Hausa, supported Dan Fodio when he began to preach against these oppressive taxations and blatant economic exploitations.

Uthman was well versed in the art and subtleties of demagogic oration. He could deliver rabble-rousing sermons that stirred the emotions of all who listened to him. He was remarkably resourceful in the presentation of cogent concerns that the populace could identify with. To garner as much support as was possible, he dabbled into the tactics of enlarging the obvious and magnifying the conspicuous. This proved very effective in stirring up strife and hatred for the ruling class.

Dan Fodio's message was singular – the solution to the myriad problems facing the general populace lay only in the immediate introduction of Islamic fundamentalism into all spheres of social engagement. Politics and law had to have their authority derived from religion. Any secular arrangement was for him a recipe for disaster. He preached that moderation in religion was the mark of hypocrisy. Fanaticism was the sure proof that you were truly a believer. Many bought into this insidious ideology, hook, line and sinker.

Soon, when he was sure that he had gained the absolute loyalty of his adherents, he began to infuse the call to jihad. Without restraint he incited the revival of the fiery fervency which had seen Islam conquer "infidel" strongholds in the past. "It was the way of Allah," he said, "to spread his religion and make it supreme over all mankind."

The advent of Uthman dan Fodio's inflammatory sermons led to a mass conversion of the Hausa and Fulani to the religion to Islam. It was attractive to convert because it assured a status of being perceived "enlightened." The promise of a paradise awash with maidens waiting to attend to your every need and fancy was opium easy for the masses to swallow. But much like all things reeking of Islamist fundamentalism/jihadism, it failed to preserve any of the antiquities of the people it converted. With careless abandon, everything that glorified the pre-Islamic era was completely destroyed. This effectively obliterated any information that could have been picked up in the composition of this compendium. Indeed, Islam was on the rampage – bulldozing everything and anything in its path to establishing a theocracy along the dictates of the 7th century Arab religion of Islam. Indeed, to buttress his message, Uthman dan Fodio soon claimed ancestral affiliations to the prophet of Islam. This claim afforded him a legitimacy of sorts in the eyes of "moderates" who could have challenged the warmongering stance adopted.

Previous reformists had concentrated on the formal conversion of pagans to the profession of Islam, (Uthman had at one time done the same–when he spent five years in Zamfara as an itinerant preacher). However, the jihad when it came took a different stance. It concentrated more on calling the Hausa to adjust their social habits in conformity with the dictates of fundamentalist Islam or be killed. The message was clear – the total domination of Islam over all socio-economic affairs.

Uthman ibn Mohammad ibn Fudi, popularly known as Uthman Dan

Fodio, was born around 1754 at a town called Marata near Birnin Kwani. He belonged to the Torankawa, a tribe that claimed to have Arab ancestry and in Hausaland was seen to be the cousins of the Fulani from Futa Toro. He is known to have revered one Alhaji Jibril ibn Umar, an expelled cleric from Gobir by Bawa Jan Gwarzo, to Agadez, in his search for religious knowledge. Indeed this celebrated fiery cleric, Jibril, was as much a teacher to him as he was definitely a forerunner. Their obviously close association spanned a period of a little over two decades (1768-1791).

Having begun life as an itinerant preacher, he sojourned at Degel in Gobir land where he was afforded the attention of more students than he had ever encountered. It is on record that Bawa Jan Gwarzo had passionately sought the friendship of this attention-prone preacher. Perhaps he figured that having this Powerball of charisma on his side would legitimize and establish his rule. The two met at Magami (an erstwhile Zamfara territory) on an Id day celebration sponsored by Bawa. But Uthman would have nothing to do with the gifts Bawa was more than willing to dole out. Instead, he demanded unequivocally for reforms in government policies prevalent at the time:

1. An end to the "exploitative" taxations.
2. The release of political prisoners along with those against whom there were no substantial evidence warranting their continued stay behind bars.
3. The right open-air preaching.
4. The non-harassment of all who chose to identify themselves with him by the wearing of turbans (in the case of the men) or the wearing of hijab (in the case of the women).

These requests were granted and the Zamfara dynasty marched out of the dungeons of Bawa Jan Gwarzo free men. However, the resuscitation of their paramount rulership in Zamfara was not resumed until much later.

In 1786, Uthman embarked on the famous five-year missionary expedition to Zamfara, during which he stayed briefly at Dauran in Zurmi and at Faru in Maradun. He was able to win a fan base from which to draw his soldiers as soon as the time was ripe to strike.

Having established a solid base in Zamfara during that expedition, he left to sojourn in Gobir. Craftily strategizing for his coup d'état using the instrumentality of religion, he began to defy Yakubu, *Sarkin* Gobir after the demise of Bawa Jan Gwarzo. Slowly, he was working towards initiating a war. But first he had to be assured that an ensuing battle between his followers (who believed they had all to gain if they died in battle) and the secularists (who did not share that fervor) would definitely result in a win for him. And he needed to justify the declaration of war. So he began inciting his followers to collectively demand theocratic rule over the secular one in existence. *Sarkin* Gobir, Yakubu, sensing the defiance in Uthman's preaching, became jittery. He had to quell the Shehu's[8] unbridled influence. And just as well, the Shehu returned to Zamfara to consolidate his hold on the rising Muslim community there, far removed from the danger of assassination. From Zamfara he went to Kebbi, and also crossing the Niger to Ilo.

In 1795, having spent five years on the throne of Gobir, Yakubu died in a battle against the Zamfarawa who in a concerted effort made another attempt to re-establish a dynasty threatened by extinction. It is certain that the freed head of the Zamfara dynasty led this battle but he is not known by name. During the battle Ali I seceded from the Zamfara city-state to form the Bukkuyum kingdom, now a local government in modern Zamfara. In 1796, Kure took up the reins of power from his father Ali I. He then conquered Danko and took up for himself as title, *Sarkin* Danko. Meanwhile, Nafata, son of Yakubu, said to have been an ex-pupil of the Shehu became ruler of Gobir.

In fear of the homage paid to Uthman Dan Fodio by a large following now that Gobir was growing weak from the incessant revolts of the Zamfarawa, the raiding by the Katsinawa (encouraged by the Zamfarawa) and Kebbi's uncertain allegiance, Nafata took panic measures to curb the seeming powers of the Shehu. He banned all forms of public preaching except by the exclusive person of the Shehu himself. He also made illegal any further conversion of any heathen to Islam forthwith, with the decree that all those who had been born pagans but had converted to Islam were to revert to paganism once more. The wearing of turbans by men and hijab by women which had served as a symbol of solidarity with the Shehu was also outlawed. A bitter cold-war was brewing. The Shehu's orchestrated excuse for the declaration of war was taking form.

2 THE JIHAD ERA

From time immemorial, Jihadists have always sought to justify their aggression towards all and sundry by citing the instance of the defense of their freedom to be the slaves of Allah and be governed by his laws, the sharia. Amazingly, the right for freedom of worship is a right they defiantly refuse others as they seek to enforce the overthrow of all other religions and belief systems to enthrone their "master" religion over all. When a jihad takes off, it stifles all opposition to its singular dictates. Even freedom of thought is outlawed. Everything and everyone must bow in submission to the rulings of clerics who control everything from the state treasury to the pulpit. Any opposing view is viewed as a challenge of the oneness of Allah, a crime punishable by summary death. This death can be by beheading, stoning, being thrown off a high building or cliff, being roasted alive, etc.

All that is needed for the radicalization of a "true" Muslim is a desire to become closer to the object of his/her worship, Allah. The trumped up assertion that radicalization is caused by a sense of alienation from westernized civilization is not true. If it were, there'd be no radicalization in exclusive Muslim enclaves where westernization is bastardized. Infighting and a parochial need for political relevance also account for radicalization. However, this is carefully shrouded in the veneer of religious duty to right wrongs in an equation where two wrongs make a right!

When a Muslim claims he is being denied rights in a society that is predominantly secular, it is laughable. Imagine a Westerner whining about a loss of rights while resident in Saudi Arabia!

Anyway, finding excuses for aggression is a mainstream characteristic of all jihadists. And Uthman dan Fodio proved himself to be no different!

In 1802, Yunfa succeeded his father, Nafata, to the throne of Gobir. Uthman had become a thorn in the flesh of his administration. He was insidiously redefining the terms of governance without having the right to – he was a guest in the kingdom, not a bona fide citizen. Secretly Yunfa plotted to assassinate Uthman. But in a society where intrigue factored into every sphere of social engagement, the plot leaked and brought the cold war that had been brewing during the last years of his father's reign to a head. Uthman, now in possession of a "valid" excuse to egg his followers on in an unprecedented uprising ordered his followers to arm themselves for "defense" now that Yunfa had "breached" security. Nothing could be done to obviate the dangers of an open confrontation now. Time alone had the eventual say.

One of Uthman's students, the rich cleric Abdulsalam, frightened by this episode fled Alkalawa. He chose to stay at Gimbana near Kebbi. Yunfa, feeling that the loss of this rich cleric would deprive him of much-needed funds (in the form of tax paid by Abdulsalam and his community), sent envoys to persuade him to return. Abdulsalam refused. Having lost face and unwilling to show himself incapable of enforcing a demand, Yunfa foolishly sent out soldiers on Gimbana to effect the forceful extradition of the scared cleric. This was in the afternoon during the month of Ramadan. Yunfa's soldiers were helped by *Sarkin* Hodi of Kebbi, whose kingdom was only fifty miles from Gimbana as against Alkalawa's hundred and seventy-five miles. Abdulsalam escaped. But members of his community were not spared. Defeated, they were marched off towards Alkalawa in the shackles of slavery. The caravan was intercepted at Degel, a stronghold of the Shehu. The captive slaves were freed and the spoils of the war returned to them. This was, to Yunfa, a flagrant defiance of his power as the sole authority in Gobirland. He was so angered that he asked Uthman to leave Gobirland with his family. Uthman bluntly refused. He cited as his reason the fear of a backlash against his followers should he leave without them. He stated that his exodus from Gobirland was only feasible if anyone wishing to do the same was allowed to do so without hindrance. Yunfa was at the end of his tether. He attacked Degel, forcing Uthman into the flight to Gudu, a place northwest of Gobirland and hometown of Aliyu Jedo, Shehu's minister of defense, on the 21st day of February 1804. The Zamfarawa seized this opportunity to appoint a new *Sarki*, bringing to an end the nearly forty-two years (since Maroki's death) of the dynastic eclipse imposed by the Gobirawa. Dan Bawa dan Gado was favored (1804-1805). Promptly, he attempted to regroup the dispersed Zamfarawa at Kurya Madaro even amidst the continual harassment from the Gobirawa. However, he managed to have a semblance of government in place because the Gobirawa were more pre-occupied with dealing with Uthman Dan Fodio. The "persecution" of the Shehu and his followers was being intensified, and the

Shehu was "compelled" into a military stance to ward off a subsequent assault. The best form of defense is said to be offense. The jihad had begun. He was elected by his followers to be their *Amir-al-mu'mi-nin* (Commander-of-the-faithful): The first to assume this noble and prestigious title south of the Sahara. At fifty, however, he was not physically fit for the tedious rigors of warfare. His brother, Abdullahi, then thirty-eight years old served as his vizier, his son Mohammed Bello, then twenty-four years old, served as one of his arch-lieutenants and Aliyu Jedo manned the war office.

Ever the dim-witted and short-sighted ruler, Yunfa was foolish enough in his desperate bid to subdue Uthman to go against Uthman at his very doorstep at Tabkin Kwotto. He camped at Ayema, half a day's walk from Gudu, before the onslaught. This encounter has been likened to the battle of Bad'r. Outnumbering Uthman's forces and possessing better equipment for warfare than them Yunfa did not even contemplate possible defeat. He was out to erase Uthman and his followers from the annals of history. But these men, armed with the firm belief that they were warring in defense of their god, Allah, dealt him a surprising blow of defeat. Unafraid to die, they fought more bravely than those who cherished their lives.

The second encounter witnessed the *Sarki* of Gummi on the side of the Gobirawa. He was even left in charge of Cimmola, four miles due south of Degel in anticipation of Uthman's advance towards Degel. At the beginning of the dry season of late 1804, the Shehu's forces moved up into the dry season pasture land near Alkalawa. Here, the Gobirawa with subscribed Tuareg mercenary support and *Sarkin* Gummi put up a counter-attack at Tsuntsua in December 1804. They defeated the Shehu, massacring nearly two thousand of his followers. Rebounding from defeat they moved down on Cimmola, chasing the supply platoon of *Sarkin* Gummi's forces as far as Kirare, near Goronyo. Faced with the shortage of food and surrounded by hostile neighbors, they traveled on, towards Zamfara territory in search of food and a friendlier environment. They passed through Kirare to Sabon Gari (sharing borders with Bakura) via Maradun in proper Zamfara territory; their advance guided by two men most familiar with the area since they were from these parts; Mohammed Tukur from Matuzgi near Mafara and Malam Dambo from Birnin Gada near Bungudu. During this retreat *Sarkin* Gobir sent out messages to other *Sarakuna* of Hausaland: Katsina, Daura, Kano and as far north as Azbin, urging them into an alliance with him to crush what he felt was a hamlet head's quest for nobility and the high-brow status of kingship. Uthman did the same, urging these men to return from the path of illusory religion to "truth." On the other hand, they need not take sides with the Gobirawa against him if they felt the first calling was too steep for them to consider, but to lend their strength to the establishment of Islam. He persuaded them to understand that it was not his intention to usurp their positions as kings of their respective domains for himself. Only Zaria responded to the Shehu's call. Aliyu Jedo had to leave the body of Uthman's retreat to forestall an ambush purportedly dispatched by *Sarkin* Katsina.

At Sabon Gari, the Jihadists built a garrison town with the permission of Dan Bawa dan Gado. Ironically Dan Bawa's successor Abarshi Dan Maroki (enthroned in the early months of 1805) was soon to sign a pact of allegiance to the Gobirawa in of an arrangement that allowed him the exclusive management of the Zamfarawa as the paramount head of the confederation of Zamfara: He sent a column of soldiers to Gobir to assist in the fight against Uthman at the latter's request. Foolishly he had plunged an already brittle kingdom into an unsavory war with the jihadists. No enclave in Zamfara was safe any longer from the jihadists who soon marched on Zurmi, subduing nearly fifty villages on their way. The hill enclave of Kanoma fell soon after the return from Zurmi. Bingi, fifteen miles south of Kanoma wa next. Jata, south of river Zamfara, followed. Twenty-two miles from Kanoma, Bini was overthrown as well.

Irked by the successful campaigns of the jihadists in Zamfara, the garrison town of Sabon Gari was constantly besieged. In April 1805, unable to discourage the Zamfarawa from these repeated raids, the jihadists turned their attention on Hodi's Kebbi. After all, he owed them a pound of flesh for his misdeeds against Abdulsalam in time past. Birnin Kebbi was taken. From here, sure of a certain amount of safety (far in excess of what was obtainable at Sabon Gari) the jihadists were emboldened to launch raids on neighboring towns that had to be captured as a matter of urgent priority to ensure adequate security and momentary peace.

The abandoning of Sabon Gari by the jihadists for Birnin Kebbi paved the way for Abarshi to occupy it as his new capital for Zamfara.

The jihadists had hoped that once in power they would enjoy some time of peace. How wrong they were! Infighting, plots, schemes and palace intrigues checkmated any semblance of peace they could hold on to. So the much-longed dream for peace in the midst of the very hostile enemies they had created remained a pipe dream. In September the same year (1805), they moved on to Gwandu. Now a neatly organized potent force, the jihadists' only snag was the persistent shortage of food supply. In other to prevent the hungry, war fatigued men, from demoralization and possible mutiny, Mohammed Bello and Abdullahi saw to the organization of a food collecting party of soldiers. From then on, assured of a steady supply of food, the Fulani jihadists went on to flatten any form of pagan opposition to their singular mission of establishing a theocratic state along the lines of Islamic jurisprudence. Flags were given to the Shehu's lieutenants as permission to initiate the jihad in their respective homesteads. That is, Mohammed Moyijo (Kebbi), Abu Hamidu (Zamfara), Malam Isaka (Daura), Malam Suleiman (Kano), Baba Yero (Gombe), Mohammed Wbi (Jama'are), Malam Yakubu (Bauchi), Mohammed Manga (Misau), Malam Alimi (Illorin), Modibbo Adama (Adamawa) and Malam Dendo (Nupe).

Peace, the absence of war, was yet to be achieved even with this smart strategy that was to ensure the eventual subjugation of the entire Hausaland and beyond. In the battle at Alwasa, Gwandu was nearly overthrown – probably because their numbers had been depleted by the exodus of the flag bearers on their respective missions. Quickly, Uthman sent for the flag bearers of Zamfara, Katsina, Kano and Daura to meet him in Gwandu to discuss the issues arising. But too busy executing the earlier strategy of conquering their stations for the Jihad these men were unable to afford heeding to the Shehu's call. In the rainy season, they got the chance, meeting with Uthman's son Mohammed Bello instead at Birnin Gada. They decided it was time to enlist the coalition of 'Yandoto, the Muslim enclave in Zamfara boasting of reputable clerics who did not share the unwavering enthusiasm of Uthman's fundamentalism. It was proposed that a round table dialog be held to iron out their mutual differences. But the 'Yandoto clerics uncompromisingly refused to grant audience to these august negotiators from the Shehu. Peeved at the outcome, the jihadists signed up for the option of declaring jihad on them too. 'Yandoto was subjugated and the flag bearers returned to their respective stations to complete their primary assignments.

Shortly after the battle of Alwasa, an uncertain period before the siege of 'Yandoto, the Azbinawa sent a force to Zamfara in search of food and booty. These booty hunters teamed up with certain Gobirawa to set Birnin Gada into chaos. Their ploy failed to displace the people of Birnin Gada, so they set off to Kiyawa (a predominantly) heathen enclave also in Zamfara. They met Namoda, a prince of the Alibawa ruling house of Zurmi. A converted protégé and lieutenant of Uthman Dan Fodio, Mohammed Namoda engaged them in a fierce battle. He defeated them. Annoyed they sought revenge by attacking Namoda's hometown of Zurmi with the aid of Abarshi. Namoda and his men barely absorbed the offensive, emerging bruised but unbeaten. This failure to win was a devastating blow to the political enemies of the Jihad, having lost substantial numbers of their forces in this engagement.

Determined to keep what remained of the Zamfara Kingdom, Talata Mafara, Bingi and Bini decided to rebel against the jihad. Then on his way to Kiyawa, Bello turned his troops against them. He camped at Wuya in Anka to map out the strategies for the coming confrontation with these "rebellious" folk. Easily he knocked holes into their ill-fated quest. He then resumed his march on Kiyawa, camping on the outskirts of Kannu.

The men of Kiyawa, on getting wind of the impending siege quickly drew support from Kannu. The siege when it began proved to be a long, tough one. More than once Mohammed Bello was forced to retreat. Only the timely twist of fate saved the day for him when under dubious circumstances the city caught fire.

The Jihad was achieving so much more than it had initially set out to achieve that it seemed the hosts of heaven were behind it all. With seeming ease, they had made nonsense of previous existing kingdoms, Zamfara inclusive. Mohammed Namoda founded Kaura Namoda when he was given a flag by the Shehu and asked to journey thence until he came upon a boabab tree standing alone, and there to make his home and domain of rulership. When he died, Mamuda, his closest kinsman present took up the rulership of Kaura Namoda. It was Mamuda who finally dealt the death blow to *Sarkin* Kiyawa, taking up the title for himself. He established Islam among the Zamfarawa who had in years past been avowed pagans.

Only six years (1804-1810) of the jihad at Gobir, Uthman dan Fodio was able to overrun a sizeable expanse of Hasaland; Birnin Kebbi and Zaria in 1805, Katsina in 1807, Gobir on October 8th, 1808 with the resultant death of Yunfa, Daura also in 1808 and Kano in 1809. In time, he was to claim places as far off as Bida and Illorin for Islam. There were no frontiers to be crossed except near east in Kanem-Bornu (and attempts were made). Kebbi, Katsina, Daura and Zaria lost their capitals and more than half their pre-jihad territories, but because their ruling houses were left intact and the capitals transferred (Kebbi to Argungu, Katsina to Maradi and Zari to Abuja), they continued to terrorize the successor kingdoms throughout the century. In 1815, Abarshi allowed his brother, crown prince Fari dan Maroki, pleni-potential powers in the governance of a battered Zamfara. Fari dan Maroki relocated from Sabon Gari to Banage, and then to Ruwan Gora. And each time he relocated, the capital of Zamfara relocated with him. During the tail end of the same year, *Sarkin* Zamfara, Abarshi, abnegated his throne to Uthman dan Bako when it became evident that he could no longer hold together his confederate kingdom no matter how much he desired to – not when the Shehu was very much around. He had always considered himself on exile and had become disillusioned by his inability to reorganize his dismembered kingdom. This event marked the end of Zamfara as the prestigious kingdom it had been in the Hausaland of Western Sudan. A new era was heralded: the eventual obliteration of Zamfara as a unified confederate city-state. Dan Bako went back to Sabon Gari to try to rebuild the ruined ex-capital of Abarshi's Zamfara. He managed to contain the feat until 1824 when he died. His son, Dan Gado, however, would have nothing to do with the sentiments associated with maintaining Sabon Gari as the capital of Zamfara. Besides, he hated the idea of being perpetually under the shadows of the past. Thus, he moved his capital to Anka in the same year of his assumption of office. He was able to exert a dictatorial hold on Anka and also force the new separate sister states of erstwhile Zamfara into recognizing Anka as the paramount state of the region. To this day, the dynasty of Anka, taking roots from Dan Bako's son, have survived all the natural mishaps that accompany a violent history.

Within a decade of the commencement of the jihad, Hausaland, down to River Benue, was for the first time under one political rule. Leadership was styled after the times of the caliphs – Uthman although still the Amir-al-mu'minin, did not, however, assume the role of a king with its attendant regal officialdom and bureaucracy. He had to prove his detractors false by refusing the mantle of kingship or risk encouraging a disaaction. All his deeds had to seem spurred and mandated by religious fervor, and not the underlying greed for political relevance that was truly the drive. So, he busied himself with a pre-occupation with the business of worship. He, however, cunningly left the little "unimportant" details of earthly affairs like grandiose state governance to his son, Bello. This enabled him to ensconce himself at Sifawa. Mohammed Bello tried several times to sway his father to reside with him at the newly established city of Sokoto in 1808. But Uthman refused. He had to keep up appearances.

After the fall of Kano in 1809, there was a need to split the empire to facilitate easy and proper governing. Uthman dan Fodio divided it into two, with Bello (now thirty years old) in control of the cardinal part in the east at Sokoto, comprising of Zamfara, Katsina, Daura, Kano, Katagum, and Bauchi. Abdullahi (now forty-four years old) was to control the west at Gwandu, a hundred miles southwest of Sokoto, but still in the Sokoto valley comprising of Nupe, Dendi, Borgu, and Illorin. Abdullahi however, stayed at Bodinga, two miles from Shehu who resided at Sifawa.

During the division of the empire, Abdulsalam showed his displeasure over being given Sabiyel, west of Gwadu, to rule. Upon Bello's intervention, he was relocated to Kware near Sokoto.

On the 8th of November 1817, the Shehu, Uthman dan Fodio died and Mohammed Bello was announced his successor; thus to bear the exclusive title of amir-al-mu'minin.

Abdullahi left Bodinga for Gwandu, unhappy at the turn of events. He had expected that being the older kinsman to the Shehu he would be nominated to the exalted office. But during these times, the palace intrigues always favored sons as heirs rather than brothers.

Abdulsalam, several years older than Bello rebelled at the latter's installation as sovereign. Driven from Kware, he was injured by a poisoned arrow in the ensuing fracas. He died at Bakura (in Zamfara) east of Sokoto.

Another rebellion roused its head at Kalam Baina near Gwandu in 1818, orchestrated by disgruntled Abdullahi boys with the sanction of Abdullahi himself, seeking to enthrone him as amir-al-mu'minin in spite of Bello. Mohammed Bello, ever the resourceful warrior, doused the revolt. The two met to reconcile and here Abdullahi formally accepted to recognize the leadership of Bello. A disastrous breach was averted by mutual tact.

Mohammed Bello, in time, proved himself a skillful administrator – what with the task of controlling a vast empire in very distant and remote places. He enforced the half-yearly payment of tributes to the office he held; wealth he used to pioneer a state treasury. With these monies, he erected walls around Sokoto and built mosques, paid salaries to a few institutionalized regular army, judges and set up a welfare scheme to cater for the disabled and the sick. Other important developments instituted were:

- The building of schools and the payment of tutors
- The teaching of the science of sugar making to his subjects
- Designating a specific area in Sokoto for animal grazing to checkmate farmer/cattle-rearers clashes
- Building a home for lepers and the blind
- Encouraging commerce and agriculture

Much of his time though, was taken up with the suppression of one rebellion or the other. These rebels against his rule had in times past been die-hard loyalists to his father, the Shehu. For instance, in Zamfara, Abu Hamidu attempted secession without success. Unfortunately, the "brilliance" of Bello's administration did not stand the test of time. At his death in 1837, at the age of fifty-seven, his brother, Abubakar Atiku, took up the mantle of power – creating a deep rift in the family. Sayyeed, Bello's eldest son had expected to succeed his father as had been the case with Bello. But Abubakar proved a better schemer in the power play than Sayyeed. Unable to contain his bitter disappointment, Sayyeed left for good to Yola where the Adamawa Fulani tolerated his cause.

The empire Uthman had so painfully established at the price of countless pints of blood soon disintegrated into large numbers of separate and often hostile emirates, loosely acknowledging the titular suzerainty of the amir-al-mu'minin stationed at Sokoto. The "nobel" ideas of Uthman dan Fodio which had inspired the jihad, and Bello's brilliant efforts at establishing good governance tailored according to the dictates of the Shari'a, had worn thin. The emirs became exploitative, raiding the towns and villages of each other in their quest for slaves; creating once again an unstable political forum.

All these upheavals of historical accidents taking place in Zamfara kingdom can be authoritatively said to have been confined to the top echelons of the social strata, i.e. the elite ruling class. The lower cadre constituting the majority of the teeming populace remained basically unchanged in their attitude of seeing themselves first as Zamfarawa before acknowledging any other loyalty (besides religion). With Zamfara hibernating, they were the pulse that kept alive the hope and craving for a resurgence.

3 THE COLONIAL ERA

The Europeans, especially the British, when they first had contact with West Africa in the 15th century AD confined their activities to the coastal areas: The spread of Islamic power over the southern and eastern shores of the Mediterranean interposed a barrier of sorts between Europeans and the rest of the world, not only in space but to a large extent mentality. However, seeing that more stood to be gained commercially and subsequently, politically, for their home countries, they began a systematic inland adventure. A little later on, their unfortunate but blatant engagement in the traffic of human cargo with the unpalatable excuse that import labor was needed for the manpower starved, recently revolutionized industries in Europe, when a multiple of their numbers unemployed roamed the streets of their capitals, is one of the dirtiest in the accidents of European presence in West Africa. This incident has been cited by certain jihadists as reason enough for the intense hatred held towards all things western. But the ironical truth is that nearly 99.9% of slave traders were Muslims. The later abolition of slavery did not go down well with them. It meant a loss of economic power. That must really be the root cause of the hatred that has festered thus long in the hearts of many an Islamist. Indeed, slavery is much an integral part of the desert religion of Islam. To brand slavery as inhuman is to simply imply that an inhuman god sanctioned it; that in itself being blasphemy punishable by painful death.

By 1897, the occupation of the northern emirates had begun in earnest under the mandate of suppressing slave raids and slavery. The British forces under Lord Luggard overran the Hausa states between 1900-1903 with Sokoto, Katsina, Gwandu and Kano among the last to give in to superior arms and strategy. In many cases, the emirs of the defeated emirates were compelled to flee from their capitals.

The colonial era had begun. This era was an exclusive period when the British through merchandise and administrative agents dominated the political arena of a subdued people. The largely Muslim populace felt peeved at the turn of events. They felt Islam was being subtly replaced by

Christianity. They felt an impotent rage against the British overlords and all they stood for. There were complaints by the Muslims of a usurpation of their "rights". Every treaty entered into was perceived by their opinion leaders to be unilateral – executed without the consent of or full regard to the rights and interests of their people.

Except for the direct pressure exerted on the traditional state of "equilibrium," which had been established between Islam and pagan societies by the brazen introduction of Christianity into former pagan enclaves, very little changed, though, in Hausaland. However, these pressures of polarity were so great that it upset the harmony inherent in this establishment before now. Indeed, no other period had seen so much impact of the comparable forces of Islamic fundamentalism and European expansion and in the end it came to a contest between the two. In May 1902, the Sultan of Sokoto sent a defiant letter to Luggard declaring, "*I do not consent that anyone of you should ever dwell with us ... I will have nothing to do with you.*" The stress and strain generated by these two potent opposing forces produced upon a relatively unstable Negro African society soon became unbearable – leading to an open confrontation. In the event the British, under Lord Luggard triumphed. Sarcastic Luggard was to comment after the sacking of Attahir on the 15th of March 1903, "*The Fulani in old times under Dan Fodio conquered the country between the Niger and Chad. They took the right to rule over it, to levy taxes, to depose of kings and to create kings. They in turn have by their defeat relinquished their rulership which has fallen into the hands of the British.*" This was almost hundred years after the first clash of the jihadists and Yunfa of Gobir on the plains of Tabkin Kwotto.

Luggard's rule did not essentially recognize kingdoms that had been obliterated by the jihad. Thus, he confined the emirates of Sokoto and Gwandu to their home territories with other sub-emirates recognizing only the religious leadership of Sokoto. He, however, saw the administrative genius of the Fulani rulers and their staff in Hausaland. It was not much different from what the British deemed to be a civilized system of governance: the administrative bloc made up of the emir, his council and the scribes (some of them were hereditary members while others were privileged favorites of the emirs). The Emir consulted his councilors on most things before taking action and more often than not heeded their suggestions. Most places had district heads and there were also village heads. These were responsible for the grassroots governance of the area under their control with no help from the outside. They were also equally responsible for the complicated tax system and its collection. There were courts to attend to legal issues and to see to the dispensing of justice. The judges of these courts were appointed by the emirs and received their wages from the state's treasury. There were also heads of markets, court poets, and people paid to keep routes safe. There was also heads of markets, court poets, and people paid to keep trade routes safe. There was also a form of police (the *dogarai*) who were simultaneously executioners, escorts, watchmen and personal guards to the emir.

Luggard utilized this bloc as the mainspring of British rule in this parts, with attempts to duplicate this system of governance over the entire amalgamated Nigeria. The attempts were an abysmal failure. But for the northern emirates the Native Administration system called the indirect rule had been born. The only modifications were almost insignificant: the councilors owed no allegiance to anyone other than the emir whose hand maintained them in office. Taxation was defined as general and cattle taxes. And the legal system and law so inextricably woven by the Islamic religion was left intact except for the introduction of the principle of appeal and the laid down channels for this. No one outside the emirate could challenge the system – and it was doing quite well even by "bogus" British standards. But it was only after a regional government had been set up and the Native Authority gotten away from the shadows of the Lagos Government that appreciable progress was registered. With this achieved, the Native Authority crept under the umbrella of the regional government of Northern Nigeria with its capital at Kaduna. Henceforth, even though the Native Authority still ran their own show as they saw fit, they needed the approval from the regional government which supervised them.

Although the Native Authorities were able to accomplish much (e.g. the construction of most of the original roads, all the elementary schools of the time, dispensaries, markets and indeed most of the social amenities with which the masses easily identify with), there was still a need for modernization and reforms to help accelerate the pace of development. And although Luggard's eminently sound political memoranda stated that *"there are not two sets of rulers – British and Native – working either separately or in cooperation, but a single government in which the native chiefs have well-defined duties* and an *acknowledged status equally with the British officers. Their duties should never conflict and should overlap as little as possible…,*" the chiefs still had an ill-defined sphere from which to operate and no one in the hierarchy was certain of his rights, obligations or powers. The people on the other hand, were still governed by intimidation and very little effort was ever made to win their confidence either by the black superiors or the white officials. The chiefs' councilors were scared of giving him unpalatable advice or adopt stances which were conflicting to his, even if these were in the best interest of development. The native staff needed a far more comprehensive training – what with district heads incapable of drafting detailed reports on their constituencies. Native treasury system and procedure needed overhauling and scrupulous straightening out. But ironically no one had summoned the courage to speak up on these ills that needed an urgent cure. In August 1950, at the House of Assembly, the "apostle of truth," in the person of the fearless schoolmaster from Bauchi, Abubakar Tafawa Balewa, moved that an independent commission be set up to *"investigate the system of Native Administration in the Northern provinces and to make recommendations for its modernization and reform with full discussion at all levels being permitted on any report produced."* As fate would have it, this revolutionary motion rather than being mowed to the ground, received an acceptance that was heralded by a standing ovation. The objective to be achieved by this reform of Local Administration when approved was that of enabling the people to take a more active role in their own administration by bringing home to them a realization of their rights and of their duties to the state. In April 1953, the Ministry of Community Development and Local Government was created to contain these pressures. Ahmadu Bello, purporting to be a descendant of the prophet Mohammed through the lineage of Uthman dan Fodio, then the Minister of Works and Communication of Northern Nigeria, was given the additional job of manning the office of this newly created Ministry – a position he filled until 1957.

Indeed, of all the great kingdoms that had reigned and declined in West Africa, Zamfara is an idiosyncrasy of sorts. Its people never let go of the will for a rebirth. And with this unyielding spirit they marched into the latter half of the 20th century having surreptitiously and unofficially inaugurated a lobbying pressure group to see to this lofty aspiration. Thus, the reforms did nothing but bring to head restlessness in Zamfara under the defunct Sokoto Native Authority: A steaming restlessness for autonomy – attesting to the fact that affiliation along the fragile lines of a common lingua franca ran only but skin deep. The more potent and overriding was clan affiliation. So as always, the people of Zamfara was themselves as a different people from the people of Sokoto although both shared the same religion, cultural values,   language   and   even   intermarried.

4 THE REBIRTH

In 1954, Chief Anthony Enahoro, a backbencher from the Action Group, served the notice of motion about self-government for Nigeria by 1956. "Saboteurs," mainly from the North, berated the motion. They said 1956 was a "too early and an inopportune time" for independence from British colonial rule because the majority of their people weren't western educated to take up the reins of western styled governance once independence became a reality. A jejune allusion given that it was the same North, in the person of the then Sultan of Sokoto, Attahiru, who had stated categorically the aversion of the Muslim North for anything and everything western in the wake of the British seeking an audience with him to forestall an inevitable engagement in war. Now the same folks were clamoring for more time to gain what they had initially rejected wholesale – western education – known in local Hausa parlance as Boko.

Sir Ahmadu Bello proverbially put the cat among the pigeons by moving for an amendment of Chief Anthony Enahoro's motion that substituted the date 1956 for as "*as soon as possible.*" A clever no deadline timeframe! Then he roped in the plausible excuse that the dynamics of the amalgamated nation wasn't secure enough, and indeed risked pushing the nation onto the brink of disintegration should independence from colonial rule be gained in 1956. He, however, "affirmed" his belief in a One Nigeria project after independence, stating that for the greater good a delayed push for independence was categorically prudent. He worked up issues of domination and marginalization in governance by a western educated South, and a possible plunging of the nation into the "unfamiliar" seas of self-government. His eloquence was enthralling and no one dared to debunk the theories he propounded with all the passion he could muster. He won the day. However, the inscrutable ways of Providence intervened: Independence was gained in 1960, just four years ahead of the 1956 date.

Funny enough, the quest for an autonomous Zamfara was plagued with a similar pronouncements. The arguments propounded for self-rule were hinged on wedges too fragile to support the weight of responsibility that would come with its realization. For instance, the much hailed economic development construction of a rail-line in 1929 through Gusau to Kaura Namoda was too isolated a case to be a primary reason for autonomy. So too were the presence of the *Sarduana* of Sokoto, Sir Ahmadu Bello, in 1938, as an officer of the Native Administration at Gusau, a district officer permanently posted here (but under the senior district officer at Sokoto) and a pathetic head-count of seventy thousand for Gusau, now the most populous district within the borders circumscribing what would eventually be the new Zamfara. Also, a crucial factor that mitigated against the bid was the sharp and fundamental differences between the historic chieftaincies; especially since those set up by the Shehu (Uthman dan Fodio) had overshadowed the indigenous chieftaincies that were inherently vital for the survival and success of Native Administration. In Zamfara, the *sarakuna* were now too independent to accept as in times past the singular leadership of the Emir of Anka. To try to force the situation would only foment chaos and rebellion. Thus, in 1962, when the people within the geographical landscape of ancient Zamfara Kingdom sought for a separate Native Authority other than the one to which they belonged, the stark disproportion and developments were the spanner in the works of the fervent agitation put up. It was a case of *sauce good for the goose not being sauce good for the gander*. Besides, Nigeria, having gained independence only two years earlier was in no hurry to make mistakes – as Sir Ahmadu Bello had succinctly voiced in 1954. And the North, fortunate enough to have been able to absorb all the educated people, leaving no unemployed class of intelligentsia, could not afford to create an arena for incompetence by the creation of a Native Authority without the availability of qualified personnel to man it. Clearly the loses outweighed the gains.

But passionately desirous of development for the North-Western Region through appropriate and judicious resource management, the region was divided into two in 1976: A move that was interpreted by political pundits as a panic measure to step up the pace of development. Sokoto and Niger were the results. But this "panic measure" orchestrated by the Late General Murtala Mohammed to spin the wheels of progress, brought to the fore the disadvantaged precipice upon which Sokoto State sat. The majority of the civil servants under the defunct North-Western Region were from Niger, so when the North-Western Region was broken up into the states of Sokoto and Niger, the officers of the administration were deployed home. The consequence was a glaring shortage of skilled manpower to manage the affairs of socio-economic administration. This inevitably led to the near economic stagnation and general backwardness of Sokoto State.

Sokoto State, before the creation of Kebbi State in 1991, was an expansive landmass defined by latitude 10° to 14° North and longitude 30°30' to 70°10' East. Among the largest states of the Nigerian Federation, it boasted of an area of 64,303.67 square kilometers, a population of 45 million and a population growth rate of 2.5% per annum. A good 80% of the populace found themselves thriving on subsistence farming, but producing enough to render agriculture the main revenue generator in the State. It was the largest producer of hides and skin, yet industries using these as their base raw materials could not thrive; owing to poor road infrastructural network in a land "too large," accompanied by the poor economic incentive drive of the indigenes. Two hundred and six kilometers away from the seat of its administration, Gusau, now with a population of 334,300 and a landmass of 3,469 square kilometers, strove for industrialization. However, it did not enjoy the encouragement from without needed to pep up the pace.

Education was in shambles. The general populace still held an unhealthy suspicion for it – alleging it turned its sons and daughters from their traditional belief patterns into anti-Islam belief patterns. Thus, with its prospective attendant economic and social trappings untapped, not much could be said of the economic emancipation of its citizens as enjoyed by other states. The morbid phobia and suspicion of western education festered unchallenged. Pedestrian "concerns" that it would turn recipients apostate since it enjoyed an overt connubial relationship with Christianity, the Western religion, was nearly palpable! Not even the quota system corrected this backwardness. It was evident that the State needed to be divided if these imbalances were to be soundly addressed: After all, the smaller a household, the more governable. But the creation of a state out of existing ones in an already saturated politico-tribal forum has its attendant drawbacks. So once these drawbacks had been thought to have been taken care of during the tenure of President Shehu Shagari, Zamafarawa sued for a state of their own; hinged on the provision of section 5 of the 1979 constitution. The participation in the agitation was very impressive. Twelve local governments appended their signatures to the petition. This time, Zamfara had a strong and genuine case, so it qualified for a referendum by the National Assembly. Unfortunately, however, "fate" with its uncanny sense of timing was not ready to usher in this development just yet. It played its hand of opposition three months into the Second Republic when the constitutional government of President Shehu Shagari was unceremoniously sacked in a coup d'état that brought Major-General Mohammadu Buhari onto the helm of affairs. But the lanky Major-General, Mohammadu Buhari, was on a mission that did not include the creation of states. So, the flames of agitation for the State of Zamfara was smothered. However, the movement for the rebirth of Zamfara stayed in the shadows on the sidelines, bidding for the opportune time to challenge the status quo.

Under the gap-toothed General Ibrahim Badamasi Babangida, the "evil genius" Head of State who seized power from Major-General Mohammadu Buhari in a bloodless palace coup, the gongs of agitation for statehood re-echoed in 1991. IBB's (as General Ibrahim Badamasi Babangida is fondly called) administration is reported to have indeed decided on carving out Zamfara along with eight others. Hopes soared high, but not for long. At the eleventh hour, Zamfara was dropped and Kebbi created in its place. The shock of this decision was profound – reverberating through the land for quite some time.

Undaunted though, the people of Zamfara pressed on with their case in the next political dispensation, under General Sani Abacha. Even though the Authur Mbanefo papers on "Boundary Adjustment and State Creation " were not made public, it is believed that they were instrumental to the rebirth of Zamfara (not as a kingdom, but as a state) on the 1st of October 1996 – its boundaries defined by an area of 28,418 square kilometers. With a teeming population of over 2.2 million, at last, the seemingly impossible feat had been achieved: The struggle for self-determination now a bold reality.

Since the realization of the quest for self-rule, Zamfarawa from all walks of life dedicatedly engaged in a concerted effort to catch up developmentally with first generation states. The task was far from easy – from whatever perspective one chose to look at it. Without a take-off grant, the pioneer Military Administrator of Zamfara, Colonel Jibril Bala Yakubu (an indigene of the also newly created state of Nasarawa), decided to employ the military tactics of imbibing team-spirit into the people he governed in an effort to achieve some level of appreciable development. With roughly seven hundred and ninety-eight primary schools and an enrollment population of a quarter of a million pupils in class attendance, western education was seen to be thriving. And with a concomitant five thousand, eight hundred and twenty-five teachers to tutor these pupils, the infidels were on the march to seduce the faithful, it seemed!

Secondary school education, which aims at making its recipients trainable in technical or professional skills and to serve as a base from which to recruit skilled manpower to fill the lower and middle level positions in public and private organizations thus gained ascendancy. The obvious higher earning power of western educated colleagues factored into "luring" hardliners to send their wards to school. The 1996/97 session boasted of a twenty-two thousand, five hundred and seventy enrollment figure. Still, though, there is a yawning gulf between the western educated class and the Islamic/Arabic educated class in terms of social prestige and earning power. To try to bridge this gulf, the Arabic and Islamic Education Board was set up. Its mandate was to tailor western education to fit into the Islamic view of subject matters, and thus make it more attractive to those who still held everything western with suspicion.

In the arena of subsistence Agriculture, Zamfara stands a titan. With over 3.5 million hectares of land under cultivation, it is no wonder that the state's original tagline was *"farming is our pride."* An annual rainfall of thirty-six to eighty millimeters, lasting from early June to October is the natural impetus Zamfarawa have needed to engage eighty percent of their population in this occupation. The problem faced by farmers due to the relatively long duration of the dry season (November-May) has being gallantly tackled by the Ministry of Agriculture. Consequently, the Bakalori irrigation scheme, which is under the Ministry of Water Resources, and the Bakura Irrigation Scheme under the state government were reactivated.

Recognition of the chieftaincy domains of ancient Zamfara was needed to be infused into the very social fabric of the new Zamfara – more a move to honor the memories of forbears. Thus, Saturday June 6th 1998 marked the official constitution of the state's council of chiefs in the epoch ceremony of staff presentation. The staffs of office were given, defined along historic lines. Thus Sarkin Anka, Attahiru Mohammed, who is the direct scion of *Sarkin* Zamfara of old was made a first class emir as befitted his station. The four others (Gusau, Kaura Namoda, Talata Mafara and Gummi) having been essentially jihadist emirates created by Uthman dan Fodio, were honored with second-class status. This meant that they derived their right to rule from the benevolence of *Sarkin* Zamfara, and thus paid obeisance and absolute allegiance to whoever occupied that office.

With the death of General Sani Abacha on the 8th of June 1998, the transition to civil rule was re-instituted by the new helmsman, General Abdulsalami Abubakar. By sheer dint of steadfast commitment to an honorable goal, General Abdulsalami Abubakar ensured elections for the various tiers of elective political offices were sequentially held; beginning with the local government elections on December 5th 1998 to the presidential elections on February 27, 1999.

On May 29th, 1999, after fifteen years of uninterrupted military rule, Nigeria was re-ushered into the corridors of democracy. Alhaji Ahmed Sani (*Yariman9* Bakura) took his oath of office as the first ever democratically elected *"son of the soil"* executive governor of Zamfara State. Here now was the crowning achievement of Zamfara reborn! Zamfara now stood in terms of self-rule, shoulder to shoulder with other sister states of Hausaland. But no! Here at last was rather the chance to play up the sinister agenda that may/may not have been behind the quest for self-determination: the imposition of Jihadist Islam in a fundamentalist agenda that sought to justify the jihad waged by Uthman dan Fodio, and in modern times abandoned by "moderate" Muslims. Project Zamfara was hijacked by jihadist elements, notable among whom was its first executive governor.

The pace of development that ensued then was proof enough that the "ideal" had been undoubtedly taken over by religious sentiments. In fact, to challenge the brewing status quo of Islamizing the state was to challenge the religion of Islam itself. Pundits of the Islamist agenda posited that Islam and politics were inalienably one and the same. To divorce them was to become apostate – a sin punishable by death!

So, all the hullabaloo that had complimented the incessant agitation for statehood proved to be just a red herrings in the game plan. Meaningless too were the words penned to the chairman of the "Boundary Adjustment and State Creation Committee:" *"our agitation for the creation of Zamfara State is motivated by no other intention than the need for accelerating the development of our enormous human and natural resources."*

5 THE DAWN

Euphoric sentiments sprouting out of independence from British colonial rule in the 60's paved the way for the drawing up of a "westernized" constitution alien to the sensitive sensibilities of the largely Muslim north. Northern opinion leaders had hoped that a constitution, "Nigerian" in make-up would accommodate a religious bias for Islamic tenets. Allowing for an "inappropriately exaggerated broad-based" constitutional draft was interpreted as a smack in the face of this lot. Strong undertow agitations for the inclusion of Muslim concerns dominated every discussion for a constitutional review in these parts. However, not much was achieved in this direction during these times. An amalgamated Nigeria was in no hurry to unscrew the bolts that held her together as one indivisible federation by massaging the inflated egos of fundamentalist elements.

In the early part of the 70's too, little or next to nothing was done entertain the "concern". Towards the end of the 70's, however, General Olusegun Obasanjo's military junta in preparation for the inevitable return to a civil rule set a "Constituent Assembly" under Udo Udoma to fashion out a workable and people oriented constitution for the country. Championing the cause of fundamental human rights, he was unwittingly encouraging the brazen call for the inclusion of Islamic bias into the letter and spirit of the constitution. Indeed, sooner than you can yell "Jack Robinson!" the proceedings of the august "Constituent Assembly" were halted when the Islamist Kam Salem on April the 6th 1978, read the formal notice of the withdrawal by about eighty-three Muslim members from the Assembly. This development was in protest to the "insensitivity" of the Assembly to respect their "just" demand that an "unbiased" provision be made in the constitution to accommodate the dictates of Islamic jurisprudence, the Shari'a – in "fair" consideration to the Muslims who incidentally made up close to half the population governed by the constitution. Not yielding to the sectarian demands of a bigoted religious apologists was construed as a ploy to foist western sponsored ideals onto a populace who were averse to it.

Thankfully, the Nigerian constitution remained secular in orientation, allowing no preeminence of one religion over another.

In 1988, General Ibrahim Badamasi Babangida, the former head-of-state who prides himself as the "evil genius," constituted yet another Constituent Assembly to draft up an up-to-date constitution agreeable to all the citizens of the country. Again the agitation for the inclusion of the Shari'a in it was side stepped, much to the chagrin of fundamentalist Muslims clamoring for the supremacy of their religion in the governance of a secular nation.

Then came 1994; and the nation fell under the firm iron-fist rule of the looting-spree head-of-state, Late General Sani Abacha. Playing to the gallery to legitimize his aberrant rule, he encouraged the incorporation of the following sections of the Nigerian constitution.

- Section 6 sub-section 5 (paraphrased) – "States can create courts and assign jurisdiction to such courts. A State House of Assembly can promulgate laws for the peace, security and good governance of their states."
- Section 38 sub-section 1 – "Every person shall be entitled to freedom of thought, conscience and religion, including the freedom to change his religion or belief, and freedom (either alone or in community with others, and in public or private) to manifest and propagate his religion or belief in worship, teaching, practice and observance."
- Section 275-279 (Paraphrased) – "Power is given to the states to make independent laws but in so far as they do not endanger a federal government."

On the surface, the inclusions were laudable. They seemingly enforced the federal character of the Nigerian State much like the U.S. where states have "peculiar" laws to address "peculiar" scenarios prevalent in their states. The downside in the Nigerian matrix, however, was that Islamists would seize such a goodwill constitutional provision to push forward their insidious agenda. And that is what precisely happened.

These sections "empowered" a legally backed Islamization of any state wishing to tread that path. This was the trump card needed by folks like Alhaji Ahmed Sani to bring to the forecourt the shadowy sentiments of Islamization later on. It came as no wonder then that on the 21st of July 1999, Governor Ahmed Sani inaugurated a committee to review the laws of the state, priming it up to the "lofty" standards of the Shari'a. Then on September the 17th, 1999, he made the historic declaration of his government's intention to implement as far as possible the Shari'a, in an epic occasion that took place at the now famous Ali Akilu Square, Gusau. This "lofty" ideal of imposing the dictates of the Shari'a on the governed in any political setting is deemed in Islam as the pinnacle of all struggles. Berated though it was from all fronts, Alhaji Ahmed Sani was deaf to all reason. He was in the middle of a cunning political maneuver from which no voice of reason could dissuade him. So on Wednesday, the 27th of October, 1999, Ahmed Sani kept his word and officially launched the Shari'a in an event that was witnessed by close to 200,000 faithfuls, gathered at the Ali Akilu Square, Gusau. Here, he mentioned the state's willingness to orchestrate the implementation of the Shari'a across the length and breadth of the Nigerian Federation. He also unveiled his fundamentalist tendencies when he announced that the state of Zamfara would gladly finance any would be mujahidin to Chechnya to help Muslims there fight infidels. Whether or not he kept his word cannot be ascertained on the latter pronouncement cannot be ascertained. But on the first, he has done "creditably" well – with the rise of Boko Haram seeking to force Nigeria under the banner of Islamism.

January the 27th 2000 marked the dawn of the so called "dispensation of light" in Zamfara state – by the now operational Shari'a. To complement this fanatical gesture, the Ministry for Religious Affairs was born. Ironically though, all these "spiritual" inclusions into 21st century governance were no more than exercises in futility. They did nothing to bring about the developments promised. But the propagandist tool of the Ministry of Religious Affairs was quick to beat the gongs of dogmatic assurances, insisting that: *"The command of Allah will come to pass, so seek not to hasten it,"* (Qur'an, Surah An-Nahl 16:1). Religion, the opium of the masses, had taken full control of Zamfara. Soon, it would awaken and embolden the militant insurgence of Boko Haram.

Yariman Bakura may have gained political clout by submitting Zamfara to the Shari'a. He also fanned the flames of Islamic dominance in the geopolitical landscape of Nigeria. Boko Haram may not be directly linked to him by way of sponsorship or publicly pledged allegiance, but the ideology held by the twain is same. Therein lies the link of complicity. Western values and education have always been seen by the Muslim mind as a standing challenge to the sanctity of Islam. And thus, with the rule of 7th century laws, society is meant to become better. However, there are no available empirical proofs authenticating this assertion that is at best a pipe dream.

Muslims everywhere, moderate or extremist, believe it their sacred duty to enthrone the dictates of their faith upon the populace within the territorial boundaries of the land wherein they have a presence. It matters not whether they are immigrants or bona fide citizens of the land under question. Indeed, failure to walk this path is to risk earning the wrath of Allah. This insidious doctrine is largely responsible for Islamic terrorism – a Qur'an sanctioned way to achieve the supreme struggle to make Allah lord over all mankind!

6 THE AWAKENING

Only folks living in denial will refute the assertion that the rise of Islamism in Nigeria is creditable to Ahmed Sani's political maneuver to manipulate the loyalties of the predominantly Muslim Zamfara electorate to his continued presence in Nigerian politics. Right after leaving office as a governor, and unable to ever again vie for that exalted position, he ensconced himself in the political fabric of Zamfara by vying for a senatorial seat – a position he currently holds. In effect, he has cleverly roped in the immunity from prosecution political office holders in Nigeria are entitled to.

Ever the controversial politician, *Yariman* Bakura, as he is fondly called, fanned the embers of his notoriety by wedding an underage Egyptian girl while a "honorable" Senator. Questioned about the rationale for "breaching" Federal child-protection laws, he calmly told the world he was following in the footsteps of the Prophet (Mohammed, the prophet of Islam had married a nine year old girl, Aisha, in a political maneuver intended to seal the eternal friendship and loyalty of Abubakar, the first caliph of Islamdom. He went further to state that he would not comply with any law(s) that sought to place itself above the dictates of his religion. Clearly, the man is a proud Islamist.

Opening the Pandora box of Islamic unrest and Jihadists agitations was seen by him and many "faithfuls" as an act of worship – one for which Allah would most certainly reward him.

Soon, other governors of the North were obliged to buy into the idea of Islamizing their states in an undisguised bid to assuage the populist inclinations of Islamic fundamentalist agitators . Gradually but surely, the seeds of Islamic fundamentalism were being sown with careless abandon!

When Boko Haram was born in 2002, it was officially christened ***Jama'atu Ahlis Sunna Lidda'awati wal-Jihad***, which means "People Committed to the Propagation of the Prophet's Teachings and Jihad." It styled itself as a legitimate response to the "ineffectual" and "incomplete" imposition and implementation of the Shari'a in the Islamized states of northern Nigeria, and what was perceived by die-hard jihadists as the gradual westernization and dilution of Islamic ideals on the national landscape. The bigoted and fundamentalist ideology held and propagated by the group was the quote from the Qur'an (Sura Al-Maida 5:44d) which states, "Anyone who is not governed by what Allah has revealed is among the transgressors." So, nationalism had translate as a rule into Islamism, and democracy jettisoned for an Islamic State framework of governance. Thus, it was far game – and indeed mandatory as an uncompromising act of worship – to oust the democratic government of the day in favor of an Islamic state with strict adherence to the stipulates of the Shari'a. Anything less was transgression and apostasy!

The headcount for Boko Haram's followership initially stood at two hundred and eighty thousand (280,000) faithfuls, with many trained in Islamist guerrilla warfare in Afghanistan's Taliban enclaves. With strong ties to Al-Qaeda in the Islamic Maghreb, the group received funding from Osama bin Laden to an estimated tune of $3 million.

Subscribing to the belief that Nigerian Muslims are mandatorily required by Allah (as an act of pious worship) to wage jihad until all territory once under the Sokoto Caliphate's rule is reclaimed, Boko Haram duly fancies itself as the successor to Uthman dan Fodio's jihad. And although the current Sultan of Sokoto is a direct descendant of Uthman dan Fodio, he currently holds only a traditional religious and tribal role, devoid of the spiritual authority Uthman dan Fodio had once enjoyed. Without the spiritual authority, therefore, Boko Haram regards the office of the Sultan of Sokoto to be un-Islamic. To worsen matters, the office is seen by them to be to too docile in the face of Western influences to command the respect it should enjoy. Any cooperation of the office of the Sultan of Sokoto and the Nigerian Federation is interpreted as proof of the desecration of the office by stooges of the West and a westernized Nigerian government.

It is not surprising, therefore, that seeking to concentrate all religious, political, economic, and moral authority in its own hands, Boko Haram views the current political disposition of the Nigerian Federation as inherently anti-Islam. Their dangerous ideology further enjoins Nigerian Muslims to feel obligated to raid the land of the infidels, occupy them, and exchange their systems of governance for an Islamic system, barring any practice that contradicts the Shari'a from being publicly voiced among the people, as was the case at the dawn of Islam. So, ultimately it seeks to foist Islamism on all Nigerians, and in time, all of West Africa – in the sure march towards the global Islamic domination pronounced in the Qur'an – making Allah's religion supreme above all else.

For them, the only paths compatible with Islam's complete dominance on the world stage are seen to be tri-pronged choices:

1. Coerced submission [conversion]

2. Payment of the jizya (a physical though not spiritual submission to the authority of Islam) and

3. The sword – for it is not legal under Islamic jurisprudence to suffer the infidel to live while he/she continually rejects submission to the lordship of Allah

The matter is summed up for every person alive: either submit, or live under the suzerainty of Islam, or die.

These inciteful blood-letting ideals, although held by Boko Haram in its entirety, did not instigate Mohammed Yusuf, the undisputed founder of the group to plunge the group into the current mold of terrorists that they now are. He was too busy enjoying the worldly comforts the jihadist donations of dollars afforded him than bother with becoming an itinerant warlord. And without the political legitimacy, he made do with preaching the faith (dawa'), much to the chagrin of his lieutenants who wanted a more vigorous and blood stained agenda: The forceful imposition of a hard and fast Shari'a. Absolutism, if you will. Brazenly, it also sought to outlaw western education – very much like Sultan Attahir had insinuated by his refusal to interact with the British.

Still, the group was a constant torn in the flesh of the Nigerian Federation's government. Open confrontations with members of the group led to the arrest of Mohammed Yusuf in 2009. Under undisclosed circumstances in the same year he died whilst still in police custody. This gave his more militant lieutenants the "legitimate" excuse to launch a military offensive against the state for "murdering" their leader – a just fight by all standards of Islamic jurisprudence.

41

Under the new, firebrand leader, Abubakar Shekau, Boko Haram quickly gained an ascendancy to notoriety by bombing churches and mosques alike. Unlike Mohammed Yusuf, Abubakar Shekau was passionately inflamed with a desire to be martyred. For him every dollar received was meant for the purchase of weapons to wage Allah's holy war. He was done preaching. Bloody action was what was required to attain the tri-pronged paths to Islamic domintation.

Soon, the gongs of war and anarchy began to reverberate across the north-eastern state of Bornu – the groups natal homestead.

In November 2012, without mincing words or shrouding intent, Boko Haram's firebrand "chief executive," Abubakar Shekau, voiced his hate on all that Islam viewed as anti-Islam. Thus, the United States of America, seen by radical Muslim elements to represent the interests of western civilization, and designated the champion of all infidel causes worldwide, became the target of his bile. He pledged Boko Haram's unflinching support for the mayhem perpetrated by Islamist terrorists in Mali, Algeria, Somalia, Libya, Afghanistan, Iraq, Kashmir, Pakistan, Chechnya, Yemen, and Saudi Arabia against American, Jewish and Christian interests. He was making it trendy in Islamic consciousness to despise the U.S., Christians, and Jews. In fact, hating anything and everything America(n) was akin to hating Jews – an act of reverent worship!

In April 2014, Abubakar Shekau announced to the whole world via a videotaped address posted on YouTube: "We know what is happening in this world, it is a Jihad war against Christians and Christianity. It is a war against Western education, democracy, and constitution… This is what I know in the Qur'an. This is a war against Christians and democracy and their constitution. Allah says we should finish them when we get them."

So consume is he by his hatred of and for the west that he has gone on to back his words with the brazen action of killing and maiming innocent, unsuspecting civilians and security forces alike to taunt her. Prior to this on February the 15th 2014, the group stormed a Christian village in Izghe, killing a hundred and six people. This was swiftly followed by an attack on a school in Buni Yadi, snuffing out the life out of twenty-nine students. In April, they kidnaped 276 schoolgirls in Chibok, later threatening to sell them into slavery in a pre-recorded broadcast posted on YouTube. The international outcry reverberated around the four corners of the world: It did nothing to appeal to their sense of humanity. In May, they went on a killing spree that claimed the lives of more than three hundred people in Gamboru Ngala.

Unflinching in their steadfast adherence to Islamic dominance, the Al-Qaeda connection has always been a source of pride for the insurgents. Abu Qaqa, Boko Haram's spokesman declared publicly in January 2012 that Boko Haram is a "spiritual follower" of Al-Qaeda. He added that "…al-Qaeda are our elder brothers… our leader traveled to Saudi Arabia and met al-Qaeda there. We enjoy financial and technical support from them. Anything we want from them, we ask."

There's been evidence to show that sometime around early August 2013; Boko Haram leaders participated in a secret conference call that included twenty top Al-Qaeda operatives, including Ayman al-Zawahiri.

All these culminated in making a U.S. Congressional report confirm that Boko Haram members have been trained by al-Qaeda in the Islamic Maghreb and that it also has potent links to al-Shabaab, al-Qaeda's affiliate in Somalia. The U.S. State Department also declared in November 2013 that Boko Haram has links to al-Qaeda in the Islamic Maghreb.

With the dwindling fortunes of Al-Qaeda; caused by the death of its chief sponsor and leader, Osama bin Laden by US navy seals in Pakistan, and the rise of the Islamic State of Iraq and Levant (ISIL) from the ashes of a destabilized Iraq and Syria, Boko Haram's leadership quickly affiliated themselves to the new game-changer in Islamism. Indeed, the ideological link between Boko Haram and the infamous Islamic State of Iraq and Levant is incontestable. But it isn't only ideology that binds these two cancers together. In March 2015, Abubakar Shekau pledged an unconditional allegiance to the Islamic State of Iraq and Levant in an audio message. In the message, Shekau said that Boko Haram "call[s] on Muslims everywhere to pledge allegiance to the caliph and support him in obedience to Allah". He added that "we pledge allegiance because there is no cure of the dissimilarity that [the] Ummah [global Muslim community] have except the Caliphate, we also call all the Muslims to join us in this goodness, because it would enrage the enemy of Allah, by Allah, our gathering under one banner, under one Imam is more heavy to the enemy." He also said that it is vital that Muslims have a leader [caliph] "that looks after them according to Allah's Rule and fights the enemies of Islam and those who fight the Rule of Allah."

Ironically, the pledge did not translate into the fusion of the two operating as a single unit. What it did was to afford the Islamic State of Iraq and Levant an increased measure of legitimacy as the sole jihadist group and by extrapolation the legitimate ruler over all Muslims worldwide.

Having killed more than two thousand people since 2009 in its unrestrained warfare, and facing defeat with the increased cooperation of the countries of Chad, Niger, Cameroon and Nigeria against it to obliterate it, a sworn allegiance to the Islamic State also served to attract foreign recruits into its fold by stamping the seal of legitimacy on it. So crass is the group's ideology that it even views disarmament to be an apostate path for consideration. Similarly, it is vehemently opposed to negotiated solutions. It is kill or be martyred – no middle ground. Abu Qaqa has said, "We will consider negotiation only when we have brought the government to their knees…we will only put aside our arms —but we will not lay them down. You don't put down your arms in Islam, you only put them aside."

In an April 2014 video, Abubakar Shekau added to the veracity of Abu Qaqa's message when he said: "If we meet infidels, if we meet those that become infidels, according to Allah, there is no any talk except hitting of the neck. I hope you, chosen people of Allah, are hearing. This is an instruction from Allah. It is not a distorted interpretation, it is from Allah himself."

Clearly he was eliminating the likelihood of a middle ground from the operations of the terrorist group. There was a concomitant increase in the upsurge of relentless military offensives, resulting in the displacement of hundreds of thousands in the wake of the unbridled offensives and suicide bombings.

A swath of land around the Nigeria, Chad and Cameroon border have been under its iron fist – showcasing to the world true Islamism – a society mired in intrigue, summary death sentences of dissident voices, an absence of freedom of thought and the relegation of women to second-class citizenship status (trumpeted as reverence to her unique physical constitution).

The gruesome murder of helpless civilians and rising body count from suicide bombing hasn't unnerved them nor sated their thirst for spilling blood. Dogmatically believing that the Shari'a is the divine law which should rule the world, they continue to kill and maim thousands in an ill-fated bid to secure their pipe dream of a caliphate for the whole Nigeria. For them no world peace is worth having until Shari'a, Islamic Law, is implemented worldwide.

So interwoven is their demands for a pure Islamic-run state with the religion of Islam that challenging Boko Haram is synonymous to challenging Islam, and by extension Allah, the god of Islam. Indeed, Muslims who fancy themselves as moderates are more often than not western educated degree touting Muslims by birth. These are the moderates who dare to speak out against the inhuman atrocities being perpetrated by Boko Haram and affiliates. And in this lies the problem: Being western educated they are seen as apostates deserving death for breaking faith with the Prophet who commanded that infidels should be forced to submit to the supremacy of Islamism. This lot (moderate Muslims) has also become the brunt of bloodletting carried out by these hoodlums of hell.

Zamfara's "noble" quest for self-rule inadvertently has brought on more harm than good for the general populace of Nigeria – no thanks to Alhaji Ahmed Sani (*Yariman* Bakura) and his ill-advised Islamization of Zamfara State. With one wave of the magic wand, the entire West African sub-region has been plunged into fear and panic. To correct this cancerous problem, the Nigerian State will have to repeal the laws backing the actions of the Islamization of the twelve northern states. This is, of course, a difficult path to travel, in the face of human right challenges that are sure to rear their heads. But if the greater good is to be achieved, sacrifices must be made – in the area of the human rights that will be "trampled" upon. Aliens to dialog, Islamists will not yield to any other course of action that gives them room to air their views and assert their "rights" to usurp the rights of infidels. With a military-backed repeal of the law and consequent outlawing of Shari'a from all states, the battle against Boko Haram and her affiliates will be won. It's the only way. Anything less is doomed to failure.

Once in force, a military style suppression of any voice of dissidence will keep Islamism tamed and tethered.

Indeed, until this bold step is taken to uproot the evil of Boko Haram by the very roots, there will be no respite for the Nigerian nation, and this diabolical group will continue to thrive in increasing legitimacy as it recruits more "radicalized" Muslims to the cause of their god, Allah.

APPENDIX

(a) LIST OF KINGS OF ZAMFARA OBTAINED FROM SARKIN ZAMFARA MUHAMMADU FAR (1928-1946) BY HARRIS P.G.

1. Dakka
2. Jatua
3. Jimir Dakka
4. Kakai Kakai
5. Dudu Fani
6. Yargoje
7. Bakurukuru
8. Bakara
9. Gimahiki
10. Karafan
11. Gatama
12. Kudandan
13. Bardau
14. Gubarau
15. Tasgarin Duru
16. Durkusa
17. Mowashi
18. Kigaya
19. Tabaran
20. Dudufani II
21. Burum
22. Burum
23. Taritu
24. Fati
25. Fati II
26. Zartai
27. Dakka II
28. Tasau
29. Zando
30. Aliyu
31. Hamidu Karima
32. Abdu Na-Makaki
33. Sulaiman

34. Mohammed Na-Makaki
35. Abdu Na-Tamane
36. Maliki (Malu)
37. Babba I C. 1715
38. Yakubu I
39. Jimira or Jinau
40. Falkar or Faskare
41. Babba II V. 1734
42. Yakubu
43. Maroki C. 1756
44. Abarshi C. 1805
45. Fari
46. Dan Bako
47. Dan Gado
48. Tukudu C. 1825
49. Abdu Fari
50. Abubakar 1829-1853
51. Mohammed dan Gigala 1855-1877
52. Hassa 1877-1896
53. Mohammed Farin Fari 1896-1899
54. Abdullahi Gado 1899-1904
55. Abdu Caccabi 1904-1916
56. Mohammed Katar 1916-1926
57. Mohammed Fari 1928-1946

(b) KING LIST OF ZAMFARA ACCORDING TO THE ANKA DISTRICT ASSESSMENT REPORT SOKPROF S.2127.F.A.K.

1. Bakurukuru
2. Bakara
3. Ginshiki
4. Argoje
5. Karafa Dan Ginshiki
6. Gatama
7. Kudandan
8. Bardan
9. Gobiran
10. Tamarin Burum
11.Bukusa
12. Mawashi
13. Kigaya
14. Tabaran
15. Dodo Fanu
16. Burum
17. Burum
18. Fatifati
19. Taritu
20. Zartai
21. Dakka
22. Tasau
23. Zodo
24. Aliyu
25. Hamitu Karam
26. Abdu Na Bawanka
27. Suleiman
28. Mohammed Na Makeke
29. Abdu Alkama
30. Maliki
31. Babba
32. Yakubu
33. Jimra
34. Falkare
35. Babba

36. Yakubu
37. Gigama
38. Malu
39. Gado
40. Maroki
41. Dan Bawa
42. Abarshi
43. Fari 1815
44. Dan Bako 1815-1822
45. Dan Gado 1822 (5 months)
46. Tukudu 1822-1829
47. Abddu 1829-1833
48. Abubakar 1835-1858
49. Mohammed Dan Gigala 1858-1880
50. Hassan 1880-1897
51. Mohammed Fari Gari 1897-1901
52. Abdu Gado 1901-1906
53. Abdu 1906-1917
54. Mohammed Mainasara 1917

(c) KRINGER'S KINGS LIST OF ZAMFARA COMPILED FROM TARIHIN ZAMFARA. *REPUTED TO BE THE MOST AUTHENTIC.

1. Bukurukuru C. 1300
2. Bakara
3. Gimshiki
4. Argoje C. 1350
5. Karafan Dan Gimshiki
6. Gatama Dan Gimshiki
7. Kudandan Dan Karafan
8. Bardan Dan Gatama
9. Gwabran Dan Kudandan
10. Taskarinburum Dan Bardan
11. Durkushi Dan Kudandan
12. Mawashi Dan Bardan
13. Kigaya Tubaran Dan Taskarinburan
14. Daudufanu Dan Durkushi
15. Burumburum Dan Mawashi C. 1536
16. Fatifati Dan Kigaya
17. Taritu Dan Kigaya
18. Zartai Dan Burumburum
19. Daka Dan Fatifati
20. Zandai Dan Daka C. 1625
21. Tasau Dan Zartai
22. Aliyu Dan Daka
23. Hamitu Dan Tasau
24. Abdu Na Bawanka Dan Aliyu C. 1660
25. Suleiman Dan Abdu Na Bawanka C. 1674
26. Mohammed Naa Makeke Dan Abdu Na Bawanka
27. Abdu Dan Suleiman
28. Usman Dan Mohammed Na Makeke
29. Babba Dan Mohammed Na Makeke
30. Yakubu Dan Babba
31. Jirau Dan Babbi
32. Faskare Dan Yakubu
33. Babba C. 1734
34. Yakubu Dan Faskare C. 1734-1736

35. Gigama Dan Yakubu C. 1739-1741
36. Malu Dan Yakubu 1741-1748
37. Gado Dan Gibama 1748-1754
38. Maroki Dan Malo 1754-?
39. Dan Bawa Dan Gado 1804-1805
40. Abarshi Dan Maroki 1805-1815
41. Fari Dan Maroki 1815
42. Dan Bako 1815-1824
43. Dan Gado 1824
44. Abdu Tukudu 1825
45. Abdu Fari 1825-1829
46. Abubakar Bawan Adam dan Dan Bako 1829-1853
47. Mohammed 1853-1877
48. Hassan Dan Mohammed C. 1877-1896
49. Mohammed Fari Gari 1896-1899
50. Gado 1899-1904
51. Abdu Caccabi 1904-1916
52. Mohammed Katar (Mainasara) 1916-1928
53. Mohammed Fari Dan Abubakar 1928-1946
54. Ahmadu Barmo 1946-1960
55. Mohammed Lawali 1968

NOTES

[1]Birnin Zamfara means "City of Zamfara"

[2]Sarakuna means "Kings" as Sarki means "King"

[3]Dan means of or "son" / "daughter"

[4]Askiya is the term for "ruler" in Gobir

[5]Mai is titular "ruler" of Kanem-Bornu

[6]Ibn is Arabic for "son-of"

[7]Na means "of" or "belonging-to"

[8]Shehu is a professorial title for a learned man. It is akin to Sheik

[9]Yariman means "Prince-of" as Yarima means "Prince"

MAPS

*NOT DRAWN TO SCALE

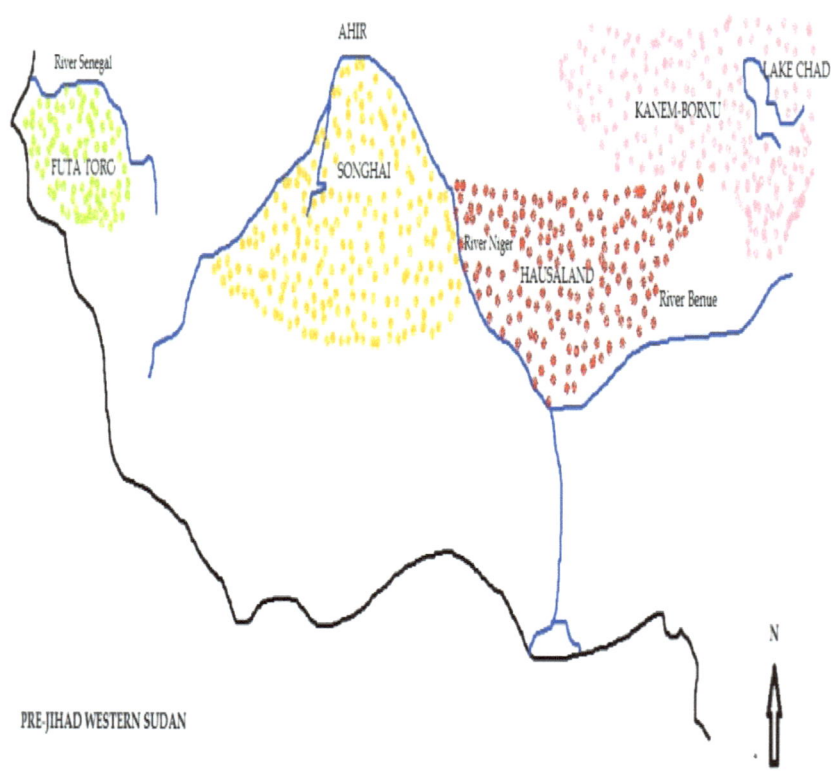

PRE-JIHAD WESTERN SUDAN

1 PRE-JIHAD WESTERN SUDAN

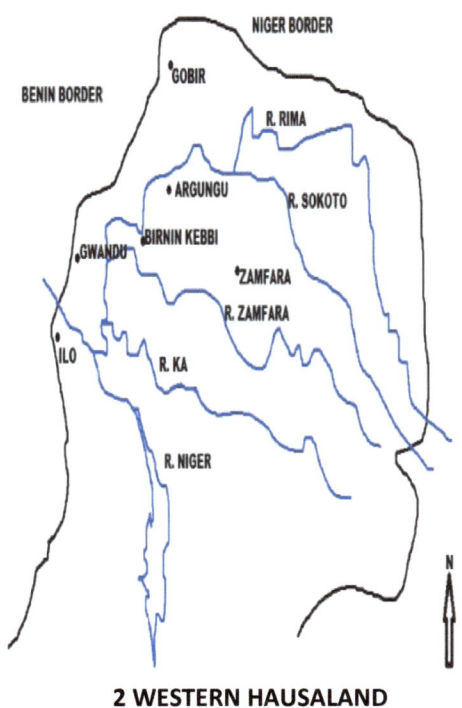

2 WESTERN HAUSALAND

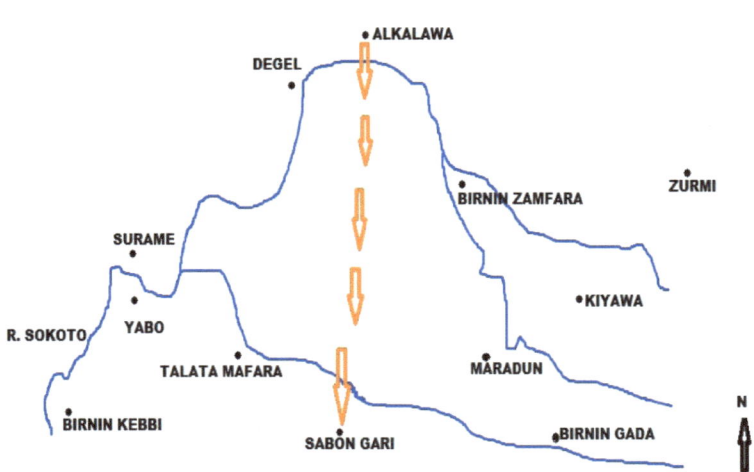

**3 FLIGHT PATH OF UTHMAN DAN FODIO FROM GOBIR INTO ZAMFARA
TERRITORY**

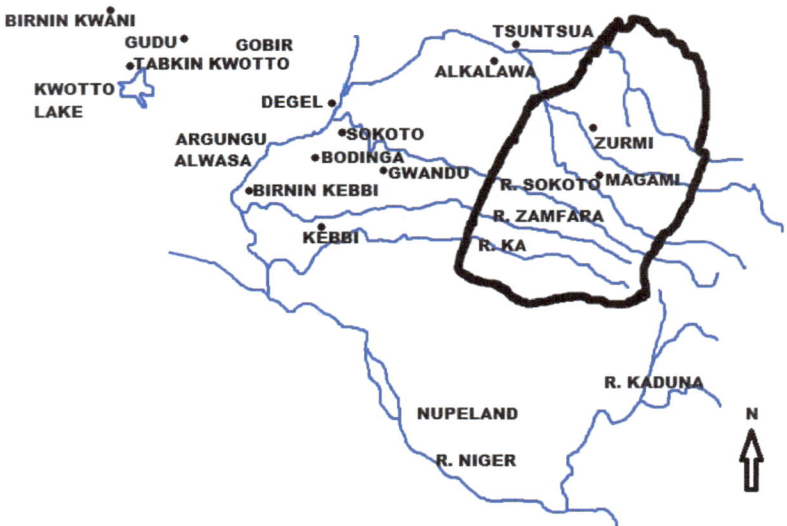

4 MAJOR BATTLEFIELDS OF THE JIHAD & ZAMFARALAND SUPERIMPOSED

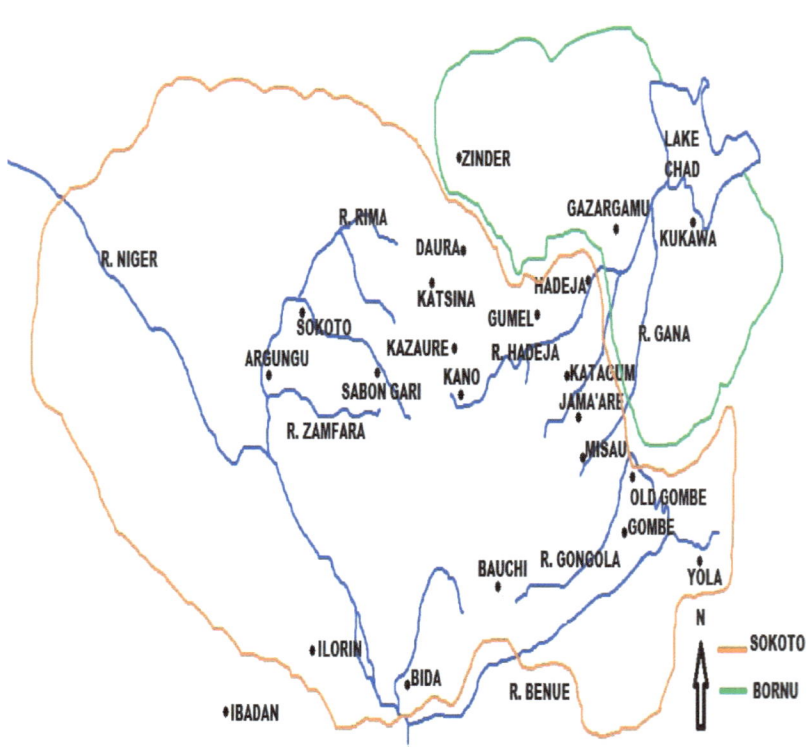

5 PRE-COLONIAL SOKOTO CALIPHATE & THE BORNU EMPIRE

ZURMI
JATA
KIYAWA
R. SOKOTO
KANOMA
KANNU
R. GAGARE
R. ZAMFARA
BINGI
N
'YANDOTO
BINI

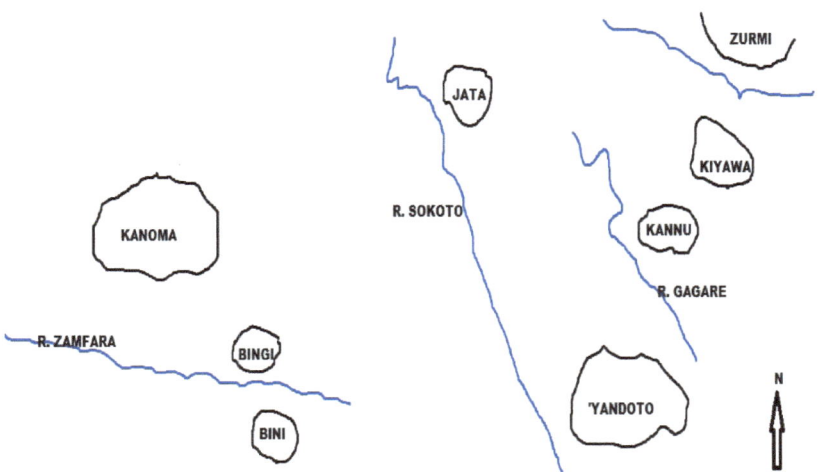

6 JIHAD ERA NORTH-EASTERN ENCLAVES OF ZAMFARA

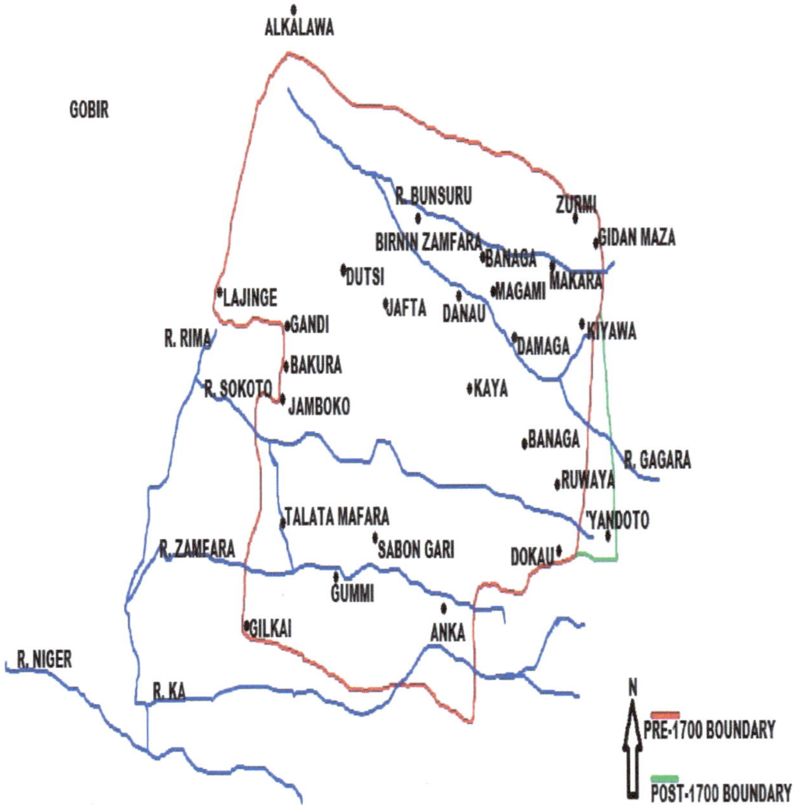

ALKALAWA
GOBIR
R. BUNSURU
ZURMI
GIDAN MAZA
BIRNIN ZAMFARA
BANAGA
DUTSI
MAKARA
MAGAMI
LAJINGE
JAFTA
DANAU
GANDI
R. RIMA
DAMAGA
KIYAWA
BAKURA
R. SOKOTO
KAYA
JAMBOKO
BANAGA
R. GAGARA
RUWAYA
TALATA MAFARA
'YANDOTO
R. ZAMFARA
SABON GARI
DOKAU
GUMMI
GILKAI
ANKA
R. NIGER
R. KA
N
PRE-1700 BOUNDARY
POST-1700 BOUNDARY

7 ANCIENT ZAMFARA

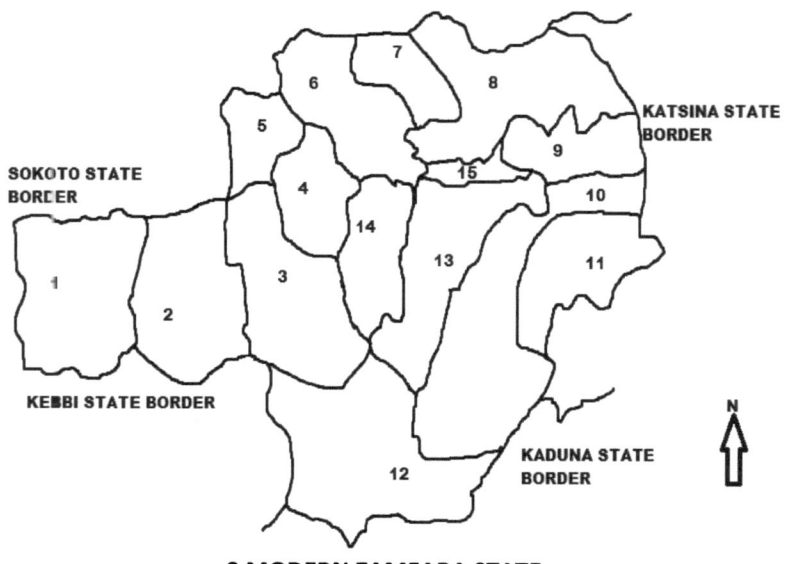

8 MODERN ZAMFARA STATE

LEGEND
1-Gumm:
2-Bukkuyum
3-Anka
4-Talata Mafara
5-Bakura
6-Maradun
7-Shinkafi
8-Zurmi
9-Kiyawa
10-Gusau
11-Tsafe
12-Maru
13-Bungudu
14-Maru
15-Kaura Namoda

ABOUT THE AUTHOR

Marxx Wells lived in Gusau, the current capital of Zamfara State before, during and after the creation of the state. During these times he wined and dined with the state's high and mighty by virtue of being a protégé of the Emir of Anka (Alhaji Attahiru Mohammed) and Governor Ahmed Sani (now Senator of the Federal Republic of Nigeria). During these times he gained unrestricted access to garnering the data herein contained – penning them with a pro-Islamist hue. However, on gaining insight into the innuendoes characterizing the agenda for global domination, he rewrote the manuscript to reflect the same and fled Zamfara for good for fear of his life.

www.ingramcontent.com/pod-product-compliance
Lightning Source LLC
Chambersburg PA
CBHW050811290526
45792CB00001B/73